Spaces to Play
More listening to young children using the Mosaic approach

Alison Clark and Peter Moss

National Children's Bureau

NCB promotes the voices, interests and well-being of all children and young people across every aspect of their lives.

As an umbrella body for the children's sector in England and Northern Ireland, NCB provides essential information on policy, research and best practice for its members and other partners.

NCB aims to:
- challenge disadvantage in childhood
- work with children and young people to ensure they are involved in all matters that affect their lives
- promote multidisciplinary cross-agency partnerships and good practice
- influence government policy through policy development and advocacy
- undertake high quality research and work from an evidence-based perspective
- disseminate information to all those working with children and young people, and to children and young people themselves.

NCB has adopted and works within the UN Convention on the Rights of the Child.

Published by the National Children's Bureau, 8 Wakley Street, London EC1V 7QE.
Tel: 020 7843 6000
Website: www.ncb.org.uk
Registered charity number 258825

ISBN 1 904787 43 6

British Library Cataloguing in Publication Data
A catalogue record for this book is available from the British Library

Contents

Acknowledgements

We would like to express our thanks to the children, practitioners and parents who have made a unique contribution to this project. We are grateful for the support of the Carnegie United Kingdom Trust and the Bernard van Leer Foundation for making this collaborative venture with Learning through Landscapes possible, with particular thanks to Gail Ryder Richardson from Learning through Landscapes and to Sue Owen from the Early Childhood Unit of the National Children's Bureau for her comments.

This work was undertaken by the Thomas Coram Research Unit, which receives support from the Department of Education and Skills: the views expressed in this publication are those of the authors and not necessarily those of the department.

Introduction

How can young children's perspectives become the starting point for change in early years provision? Working with three- and four-year-olds in a preschool in the United Kingdom, this pilot study set out to explore with young children their understandings and uses of outdoor provision, in order to inform future plans. Three key themes have emerged: the importance of listening to young children about their environment; the links between listening and learning; and the possibilities and challenges for research on listening to young children.

One of the findings of research by the Carnegie Young People's Initiative states the following:

> Start early and start locally. Adults very often underestimate the capacity of young people to become involved — higher expectations are needed. It is important to begin to develop a habit of involvement much earlier. Schools and neighbourhood are the most important sites for involvement ...
> (Cutler and Frost 2001)

It is for this reason that this project has focused on introducing children early to the processes of decision-making. We have chosen a local context, the outdoor space attached to a preschool. Our methods have been an adaptation of the Mosaic approach. We believe this provides a framework for raising expectations of what young children can contribute. This is a strength-based model for listening to young children that we developed (Clark and Moss 2001), based on earlier research supported by the Joseph Rowntree Foundation. Starting with a view of the competent child, the Mosaic approach combines traditional research tools with participatory methods in order to listen to the views and experiences of young children.

This book sets out to:

- explore how to listen to young children's views and experiences of their outdoor environment, in order to inform change
- describe the adaptation of the Mosaic approach to work with young children in outdoor spaces
- demonstrate young children's competencies in expressing their perspectives
- discuss challenges and future directions for practitioners and researchers in listening to young children.

The Spaces to Play pilot project described in this book has been funded by the Bernard van Leer Foundation and the Carnegie Trust. Focusing on the outdoor environment, the project has been carried out in collaboration with Learning through Landscapes, the school grounds charity. The research has been undertaken in one of 15 settings in Kent participating in the Spaces to Grow project organised by Learning through Landscapes.

Part One provides the context for this study, beginning with three questions:

- What is our view of the child?
- What do we mean by listening?
- Why should we consider children's views on the outdoor environment?

Part One includes a review of literature with key texts from early education, environment education, childhood studies and children's participation.

Part Two describes the Mosaic approach in action in a preschool in the UK. The focus here is on a practical explanation of the process as well as the outcomes. Details are provided of the different research tools used with young children, early years practitioners and parents, and of the children's insights about their outdoor spaces. Part Two ends by illustrating how the material gathered provided the starting point for change.

Part Three discusses the challenges and possibilities raised by this study for using this approach more widely. This will include three key elements:

- messages for practitioners using the Mosaic approach to make changes to the outdoor environment
- messages for practitioners linking the Mosaic approach and learning
- messages for researchers using the Mosaic approach with young children.

Part One:

Background

A study about listening to young children poses challenging questions for researchers and practitioners. Before going into detail, it is important to make clear our starting points for this study; our assumptions and expectations about young children; our understandings about listening; and our focus on the physical environment. This part concludes with an introduction to the Mosaic approach.

What is our view of the child?

Our first starting point relates to our view of the child and childhood. How we 'see' young children is influenced by our culture, our training, the theories we hold, and our experiences as children and as adults.

The following terms describe how we view children in our research:

- young children as experts in their own lives
- young children as skilful communicators
- young children as rights holders
- young children as meaning-makers.

Young children as 'experts in their own lives'

This phrase used by a Danish colleague (Langsted 1994) describes our view of children as competent commentators on the details of their everyday lives. This view acknowledges the unique perspective children can communicate about their own lives. This is not to ignore the views of adults, but is intended to focus adult discussions on children's perceptions and priorities.

This view of children has been influenced by the emerging field of the sociology of childhood. This supports the view of children as 'beings not becomings' (Qvortrup 1994), 'who have their own activities and their own time and their own space'. This emphasis on the present lives of children rather than on how they might develop has particular importance when thinking about young children. Too often, young children have been seen as incomplete individuals who need to be prepared for the next stage. Qvortrup comments: 'children [are] often denied the right to speak for themselves either because they are held incompetent in making judgements or because they are thought of as unreliable witnesses about their own lives'.

Researchers working within the field of the sociology of childhood have used this starting point to document children's own perspectives on different aspects of their lives (for example, James and Prout 1997; Mayall 2002), including the views of young children (Brooker 2002; Clark, Moss and Kjørholt forthcoming).

Young children as skilful communicators

This view of the child emphasises children's abilities to express their views and experiences. It is one of the four 'aspects' chosen in the *Birth to Three Matters* guidance (Sure Start 2002) to 'celebrate the skills and competence of babies and young children' (David and others 2002).

Malaquzzi, the founder of the preschools of Reggio Emilia in northern Italy, referred to the 'hundred languages of children' (Edwards and others 1998). These preschools promote the myriad ways young children use to communicate using all their senses. This idea of competency places a particular emphasis on the role of the adult. The focus is on adults supporting young children to communicate their perspectives by providing a rich array of different resources and environments. This is in contrast to seeing young children as poor communicators who present adults with great difficulties in understanding their wishes and feelings.

The view of children as skilful communicators applies to children with a variety of abilities. More imagination, patience and skill may be required by adults to support some children with special needs. However, the question is not whether children have any knowledge to convey but how hard we work to make sure every child has the opportunity to share their point of view (for example, Dickins and others 2003; NSPCC/Triangle 2004). Issues relating to listening to babies, listening to disabled young children, supporting parents to listen and listening to young children about equality issues are the focus of a series of leaflets: *Listening as a Way of Life* (Clark 2004; Dickins 2004; McLarnon 2004; Rich 2004; Road 2004).

Young children as rights holders

This view of the child has been upheld by the United Nations Convention on the Rights of the Child. This is an active view of childhood, which recognises the status of children now as well as in the future. The Articles within the Declaration deal with children's rights in three broad categories (Lansdown 1996): the right to protection from harm, to provision of services such as healthcare and education, and the right to participation.

Two of the Articles are of particular importance when discussing listening to young children. Article 12 declares that children who are capable of forming their own views have the right to express those views freely in all matters that affect them. Article 13 presents the right to freedom of expression and specifically details the range of media that should be open to children to receive information and to express their ideas: 'either orally, in writing or in print, in the form of art, or through any other media of the child's choice'.

These Articles represent children's rights not only to be given space to express their views but also to be given access to and experience of using a range of different methods in order to do so.

Young children as meaning-makers

This view of the child sees young children as active participants in their own learning. This is in keeping with a constructivist view of learning as a collaborative process between adults and children and between children and their peers (for example, Bruner 1985; Vygotsky 1978). If young children are acknowledged as playing an active part in a search for meanings, then their own perspectives on this learning process become of paramount importance (Brooker 2002; Carr 2000; MacNaughton 2003).

What do we mean by listening?

Our second starting point relates to our understandings of listening. There has been increasing policy, research and practice interest in listening to and consulting with young children (Clark 2003, 2004; Clark and others 2003; Clark and others forthcoming; Lancaster 2003). It becomes more important at such times to be clear about what we mean by listening and consultation.

We searched for definitions of these terms in our review of the field of listening to and consulting with young children (Clark and others 2003). We concluded that listening might be understood as:

- an active process of communication involving hearing, interpreting and constructing meanings
- not limited to the spoken word
- a necessary stage in participation in daily routines
- participation in wider decision-making processes.

There are different types of listening that might involve young children in an early childhood institution, including:

- everyday listening by those who regularly work with young children, giving opportunities for decision-making in routines and activities
- consultations about a particular issue, event or opportunity.

Consultation involves listening, but is listening with a particular purpose. Borland (2001) describes consultation as 'ways of seeking the views of children as a guide to action'. Both listening and consultation may lead to action but consultation begins with a fixed objective in mind.

Why should we consider young children's views of the outdoor environment?

Our third starting point relates to children's engagement with the outdoor spaces. This section sets out a brief outline of some of the relevant work to show why debates around young children, participation and the outdoor environment need to go together.

Children's participation in their local environment

Children's participation in issues relating to their local environment has been encouraged by global concerns about the future, as expressed at the UN Conference on the Environment and Development in 1992. There is a heightened policy interest in this area. The Mayor of London's Children and Young People's Strategy and the State of London's Children reports (Hood 2001, 2004) are but two recent indicators of this growing policy interest in children and their environment in England.

Children's active involvement in changing their environment has also been promoted by a number of key projects exemplified by the UNESCO Growing up in Cities project (Chawla 2002). This initiative, begun by Kevin Lynch, offered one of the first cross-cultural explorations of young people's perspectives on the environment. The Growing up in Cities project has produced numerous documented examples of children's involvement in community development and has also developed a manual for children's participation in this area (Driskell 2002).

Other practical guides to children's involvement in environmental planning include the comprehensive volume by Hart (1997), which has a detailed methods section. Two important examples from practice in the UK include Adams and Ingham (1998), who present case studies of children and young people's involvement in environmental planning across a range of contexts, and the Children's Play Council, which outlines ways of carrying out play space audits that acknowledge children 'as the primary experts in play' (2002).

Studies of children's play can provide a rich source of information about children's knowledge of their local environment. *Children's Experience of Place* (Hart 1979) is a classic example of how detailed ethnographic study has revealed children to be knowledgeable, competent users of their local environment. More recent studies have examined children's perspectives on their play environments, including out-of-school-hours play centres (for example, Petrie and others 2000; Smith and Barker 1999). Burke (2002) looked at play opportunities in East Leeds, where children aged 7 to 11 years old made photographic diaries for one week, to show the spaces and sites they used for their everyday play activities.

Children's participation in their school outdoor environment

Children are the primary users of school outdoor spaces. Titman (1994) highlights the significance of school spaces for children as the first public environment in which children can feel themselves to be stakeholders. Increasingly, children have been encouraged to be involved in planning changes to their school grounds. Learning through Landscapes (begun in 1990) has been one of the prime catalysts for involving children in this way. Rowe (1991) describes children as active participants in the process of change. This emphasis has continued in more recent work: 'Pupils make real decisions about changes that will affect them, help in the completion of those changes, are involved in the maintenance and in the evaluation of their success' (Learning through Landscapes 2000).

Adams and Ingham (1998) include case studies of children's participation in changes to school grounds as examples of children's involvement in environmental planning.

Young children's participation

Young children's effective participation presents policy-makers, academics and practitioners with difficult challenges. One stumbling block can be knowing what methods are appropriate for listening to young children's views and experiences. A second issue relates to how these perspectives can inform changes to policy and practice.

There have been a small number of studies in which these barriers have been overcome. These studies demonstrate young children's abilities to provide new insights on subjects they are familiar with, such as their early childhood institutions (for example, Clark and Moss 2001; Cousins 1999; Daycare Trust 1998; Dupree and others 2001; Lancaster 2003; Miller 1997). Research to date indicates a number of key factors that young children have identified as important to their enjoyment of their early years provision. This has included access to the outdoor environment (for example, Driscoll 2004) and, in particular, use of favourite equipment and hidden places (for example, Clark and Moss 2001).

A range of methods has been recorded for listening to young children's views and experiences (see Clark 2003). Some traditional techniques, such as interviews and questionnaires, have been adapted from consultation work with older children and adults. The use of arts-based activities, such as photography, have opened up new possibilities for gathering young children's perspectives (Clark 2003; Clark and Moss 2001; Daycare Trust 1998; Driscoll 2004; Lancaster 2003).

■ Young children's environments

The immediate environment played an important part in the history of early years provision. Margaret McMillan, one of the champions of nursery education in the UK in the early twentieth century, promoted the importance of outside space for young children (Dudek 2000; McMillan 1919). Even the term 'kindergarten' derives from the idea of a nursery as a metaphorical garden. The outdoor environment has been an important element in nursery design throughout the nineteenth and twentieth centuries.

Early childhood experts have emphasised the importance of the physical environment for the well-being of children (for example, Bilton 2002; Ouvry 2003; Perry 2001). This is emphasised in the Foundation Stage curriculum guidance for England, for children aged three to six years, which states: 'Well planned play, both indoors and outdoors, is a key way in which children learn with enjoyment and challenge' (QCA 2000). This curriculum guidance includes Early Learning Goals that are pertinent to the subject of young children's environments. For example, one of the six learning areas, 'knowledge and understanding of the world' contains an Early Learning Goal to develop 'the sense of place' which encourages children to explore their local environment, make maps and models, and discuss their likes and dislikes.

The preschools of Reggio Emilia in northern Italy are worthy of special mention in this context. A founding principle of these is the view of the child as competent and strong, a 'rich child' (Rinaldi 2001a). The environment has been described in these preschools as being 'the third teacher', with indoor and outdoor spaces being seen as active ingredients in the learning process, rather than passive structures.

There have been a small number of published studies that have involved young children as active participants in the planning of their outdoor environment. Stirling Council (2000) offers an example of how local authority commitment to encouraging the fullest possible use of the outdoor environment, together with a strong belief in listening to young children, can enable young children's perspectives to make a difference.

The Story Garden at the Discover Centre in East London (CABE Space 2003) offers another inspirational example of how taking children's views seriously can lead to imaginative play spaces that children can enjoy, transform and renew.

This review demonstrates the range of work that is of relevance to a study of young children's participation in their outdoor environment. As more children attend 'preschool' services, attention to outdoor space and children's involvement in planning such space shifts to younger ages. Hence the focus of this study is on the possibilities for involving younger children in outdoor environments.

Introduction to the Mosaic approach

We developed the Mosaic approach as part of a research and development project to explore new ways of including the 'voice of the child' in reviewing services. We will refer to this work as 'the original study' to distinguish it from later developments. This was part of a wider study to evaluate a multi-agency network of services for families and children (Wigfall and Moss 2001). A detailed account of the development of the approach has been written elsewhere (Clark 2003; Clark and Moss 2001). This section offers a brief summary of the approach and its component parts.

The Mosaic approach enables young children to create a 'living picture' of their lives. It brings together a number of research tools, both traditional and participatory, in order to explore and listen to young children's views and experiences. These tools are chosen to 'play to young children's strengths, methods which are active, accessible and not reliant on the written or spoken word' (Clark and Moss 2001). Explicit in the approach is a belief in young children as competent commentators. The approach places children's perspectives at the centre of discussion with adults.

There were two stages to the Mosaic approach in the original study. Stage One involved using the tools to gather and document children's and adults' perspectives. This data-gathering phase is followed by Stage Two: piecing together information for dialogue reflection and action.

A mosaic is an image made up of many small pieces, which need to be brought together in order to make sense of the whole. The Mosaic approach gives young children the opportunity to demonstrate their perspectives in a variety of ways, calling on their 'hundred languages' (Edwards and others 1998). Each tool, such as the cameras, the tour and map-making, provides a piece of this overall picture. One or two tools together may give an insight into children's interests and priorities. However, bringing together a range of tools may give a more detailed impression of young children's perspectives.

Table 1.1: Tools used in the Mosaic approach

Method	Comments
Observation	Narrative accounts
Child conferencing	A short structured interview schedule, conducted one-to-one or in a group
Using cameras	Children using cameras to take photographs of 'important things'
Tours	Tours directed and recorded by the children
Map-making	2D representations of the site using children's own photographs and drawings
Interviews	Informal interviews with practitioners and parents

Stage One

Observation

The first tool is observation. This forms the starting point for the direct work with young children. Observation is an important first step in listening to young children's views and experiences. The younger the children involved, the more important observation becomes for increasing the researcher's understandings of children's perspectives. We use a qualitative framework for observation, which takes the form of narrative accounts. These are written descriptions of episodes of children's play recorded during a half-day or full-day period. Observation provides the foundation for the participatory tools.

Child conferencing or interviewing

Within the Mosaic approach, child conferencing provides the opportunity for formal conversations with children about their present early childhood institution. Structured interviews are based on a schedule developed by the Centre for Language in Primary Education, London, in the 1980s. The open questions ask children why they come to their nursery, what they enjoy doing or dislike or find hard. Some questions focus on important people, places and activities. These questions can be adapted to fit different contexts for listening. There is the opportunity for children to add other information they think the interviewer should know about their institution. These interviews can be conducted 'on the move' by children taking the researcher to the places in question.

Cameras

Cameras provide a participatory tool through which young children can communicate. A number of recent studies have incorporated the use of cameras with older children (for example Burke 2003). This silent tool has great potential for use with young children (Entz and Galarza 2000). Children are asked, in the Mosaic approach, to take photographs of important things and important places in their early years provision. The original study used disposable cameras. These have proved to be effective tools for young children to operate; however, digital technology offers other possibilities. The young photographers demonstrate their competency and delight in handling the cameras. Taking photographs and looking at the results provides a platform for talking and listening. The children were given their own set of the photographs, from which they selected photographs to make their own individual books about their nursery.

Tours and map-making

Tours and map-making are tools that follow on from the use of the cameras. Tours are a participatory technique, similar to the idea of 'transect walks', which have been used in international development programmes for people to convey their local knowledge about their immediate surroundings (Hart 1997). Neighbourhood walks have also been used to involve children in environmental planning (Adams and Ingham 1998). Langsted (1994) describes a similar approach in the BASUN Project, a comparative study of the daily lives of young children in five Nordic countries. Each five-year-old took the researcher on a 'sightseeing trip of his/her daily life'.

The physicality and mobility of this technique lends itself to being used by young children. This tool plays to their strengths as natural explorers and knowledgeable guides. The 'normal' power balance in the classroom is reversed and children are in control of the content of the tour and how it is recorded.

Map-making brings together material children have gathered from the tours. Hart also describes the use of child-made maps as follows:

> The method can provide valuable insight for others into children's everyday environment because it is based on the features they consider important, and hence can lead to good discussion about aspects of their lives that might not so easily emerge in words.
> *(Hart 1997)*

We have found young children can use maps made of their own photographs and drawings as another way of expressing their feelings about their environment. These maps can also be an interesting talking point for other children and parents.

Interviews with practitioners and parents

Interviews with practitioners and parents build up a more detailed understanding of young children's experiences. Their insights about the children can add an important dimension to discussions of children's perspectives, raising areas of consensus and perhaps disagreement. This can form the basis for more listening to children to understand how they interpret the world. Excluding adults' voices could run the risk of disenfranchising adults who may themselves have limited opportunities to express their opinions.

■ Stage Two

This second stage acknowledges the role of children and adults in discussing and interpreting meanings. The visual nature of some of the material gathered, for example the children's photographs, books and maps, helps to facilitate dialogue between young children and adults, starting from the child's point of view. Discussions took place, in the original study:

■ between practitioners and the researcher
■ between children and the researcher
■ between parents or parents and children together and the researcher
■ between practitioner groups and the researcher.

We describe this process as 'meaning-making', in which young children play a central role, making sense of or interpreting what this detailed and varied material can tell us about their lives.

Documentation as a process allows these discussions to be open: parents, for example, can be shown photographs, hear children's responses to the interview questions and look at the children's maps. As Carlina Rinaldi (2001b) describes it: 'Documentation is visible listening'.

We have sought in this section to introduce our rationale for focusing on listening to young children about their institutional outdoor space and to outline the Mosaic approach, which we adapted for this pilot project.

Part Two gives a detailed account of the practicalities of making visible young children's knowledge and understandings of their environment in order to inform change.

Part Two:

Spaces to Play

This section will provide a detailed account of how we adapted the Mosaic approach to listen to young children about their outdoor environment. We will begin with a brief description of the project and the preschool, followed by an exploration of the process. The section ends with an account of the changes that a dedicated team of parents have brought about, influenced by the children's perspectives.

This pilot project, Spaces to Play, is informed by two earlier pieces of research. First, the original project outlined in Part One, to gather children's views and experiences of their early childhood institution. Spaces to Play focuses on the outdoor environment and investigates the usefulness of the Mosaic approach as a group tool in addition to its application with individual children.

The second piece of relevant recent research has been a literature review for the Department for Education and Skills, *Exploring the Field of Listening to and Consulting with Young Children* (Clark and others 2003). This indicated the paucity of studies based on young children's views of their immediate environment.

The Spaces to Play project has been carried out in collaboration with Learning through Landscapes, and is part of their Kent 'Spaces to Grow' project. Learning through Landscapes is a voluntary sector organisation that works with schools to promote the design, use, development and maintenance of their grounds. The organisation has a long track record in including children's views about their outdoor spaces and in supporting research (for example, Titman 1994).

The Kent 'Spaces to Grow' project has been an opportunity for Learning through Landscapes to develop their early years work in partnership with the Kent Early Years Development and Childcare Partnership. Fifteen early years settings across the county were given small grants to develop accessible, replicable, low-tech, low-cost and affordable solutions to the barriers preventing development of their outdoor environment. The planned changes were to be in keeping with the National Standards for Under Eights Day Care and Childminding (standard 4.11: 'normally, outdoor play space adjoining the premises is provided'), the Foundation Stage curriculum requirements (QCA 2000) and the Kent Quality Kitemark. These projects were planned to provide demonstrations of good practice and inspiration for all other early years settings in Kent. The Spaces to Play project took place in one of these 15 settings.

 Spaces to Play project

The pilot project's overall aim was to demonstrate how children under five can contribute to the decision-making processes concerned with changes to outdoor play provision.

We selected a preschool on the outskirts of a small town in Kent to be our case study. This is one of the settings taking part in the Spaces to Grow project. The manager and practitioners had therefore identified themselves as wanting to develop the outdoor provision and had been given a small grant from Learning through Landscapes to begin this process.

The preschool has over 80 children on roll with up to 36 children at each session. The preschool is a 'Special Needs' resourced nursery so a number of the children have a range of special physical or behavioural needs. The preschool serves an area of economic disadvantage. It had recently had to move to a new site and was housed in a 'portacabin' on a plot of land situated in a local authority park. The preschool outdoor space was on a corner of this plot of land, separated from the park by a 'vandal-proof' fence.

The pilot project took place between September 2003 and February 2004. Twenty-eight children, aged three to four years old were involved, together with parents and practitioners. The fieldwork, carried out by one of us, Alison, included 11 full-day visits and two half-day visits to the preschool.

Outdoor play at the preschool
(Photo by Gail Ryder Richardson)

We were keen to involve as many children as possible in the project. The first step was to explain the research to the preschool manager, to confirm her interest and to gain her consent. Next we sent a letter to the parents introducing the project. This letter included a consent form to gain the permission of the parents for their children to take part. In addition to this parental consent, the children were asked on each occasion they worked with Alison whether they wanted to be involved on that day or not.

It was important to allow time for a familiarisation visit where the children and practitioners met the researcher in an informal way. Alison spent the day following the children through their routines, whether outside or inside.

Figure 2.1: Individual pieces of the Mosaic approach

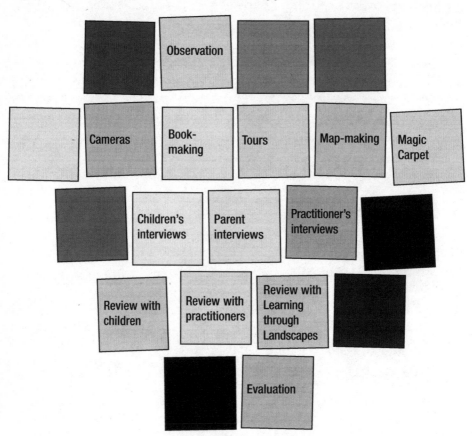

The Spaces to Play project was about listening to young children with a practical purpose – to inform change to the outdoor space. We decided to add a third stage to the Mosaic approach in order to make explicit this decision-making element. This last stage focuses on how children's perspectives can form the basis for action – whether this is positive decisions to protect areas of interest or to change.

- Stage One: gathering children's and adults' perspectives
- Stage Two: discussing the material
- Stage Three: deciding areas of continuity and change.

Figure 2.1 shows the different pieces of the Mosaic approach which we used in this pilot project.

We will begin by describing Stage One: gathering children's and adults' perspectives. This involved a range of tools: observation, then the participatory tools of cameras, book-making, tours and map-making. We introduced a new tool at this point, the Magic Carpet, to promote conversation with children about their wider environment. Stage One includes more formal opportunities for listening and talking through the interviews with children, parents and practitioners.

This section will describe both the process of using the tools and an indication of the insights we gained.

Stage One

Observation

The observation was carried out over three days. The aim of the first day was to gain familiarity with the preschool and its routines, together with a general feel for how the children used the outdoor space. The following week, two focused, all-day observations were carried out.

Two techniques were used for these in-depth observations. First, we made narrative accounts using non-participant observation of five children, two girls and three boys. These children were chosen at random from the group of children whose parents had given permission for them to be involved, to include both genders. We supplemented the written notes by taking photographs. Second, we conducted short, timed observations of the use of the house and the soft play surface. These areas had emerged as popular play spaces from the general observation and seemed to warrant closer investigation.

Figure: 2.2: What the use of observation revealed about children's use of place

---

Large play equipment

House – a social place; for being noisy, talking and singing, imagining

Caterpillar – a social place/physical space for jumping, balancing

Logs – balancing

Compost tray – the lid is a social place

Inside sand pit – a social place for relaxing, digging, talking

Play surfaces

Decking – a social place, for talking, balancing objects, manipulating pieces, constructing

Soft play surface – a physical space and a social place for individual games and group play

Slope and grass – not in use

Other places

Portacabin wall – investigating a spider climbing up the wall

Beyond the fence – watching

Observing the children's use of the outdoor space revealed a number of important places where children gathered (see Figure 2.2). This information provided the starting point for using the other tools.

Soft play surface

The main section of the outdoor play space in regular use had been covered in a rubberised surface. This provided a smooth and safe surface for riding bikes, cars and the scooter, and a base for the climbing frame. At first this appeared to be a popular space for energetic play, children dashing about from corner to corner. Closer observation showed the complex social networks, talking and role-play that the children were also engaged in.

Figure 2.3: Excerpt from researcher's field notes

Two girls are playing together. One is in a toy car and the other is on a tricycle.

Julie (on the tricycle) to Jane: Do you want to swap with me and have some fish and chips?

Jane: No reply

Julie: Do you want to go on that bike?

Jane: No reply

Julie: Look at your lovely car. Did you get it from the garden centre?

Jane: It's from the hospital

Julie: Ohhh, it's a hospital person's car. Where do you want to go?

Jane: To the ships.

Julie: Do you want to go to the zoo? Let's go …

Julie to Ruth: Do you want to go to the zoo? Let's go.

Timed observations revealed a fluctuating use of the soft play surface during the session. This reached a peak of 13 children at 10am (more than a third of the children present that morning), which dropped to five children by 11.10am.

Decking

An area of the outdoor space had been covered in wooden planks as the first part of changes to the outdoor space. This covered approximately a quarter of the ground area in current use. A plastic table and benches were placed on the decking. Drawing activities or puzzles were in use on the table. Several times during the day children would play a board game with an adult sitting at the table or sitting together on the decking. The floor space also provided a flat surface for construction toys.

The observation revealed the decking area being used in several ways by different children. At times it provided a quieter space where children could go if they wanted to be with an adult. At other times this was a building space, where children could go and work on a sustained piece of construction without needing to tidy anything away.

Figure 2.4: Excerpt from researcher's field notes

Two boys are using the construction bricks

Henry: Let's do a big tower.

Colin: I'm not yours anymore …

Henry: I'm staying to lunch anyway.

Colin: So am I.

Henry: Let's do a big one, massive … we need one of these [a board] underneath.

Colin: I'm doing a jigsaw.

[Colin proceeds to place square and rectangular bricks together on the board to make a jigsaw and Henry continues to build his tower.]

The slope and the grass

The outdoor space is surrounded by a steep slope that leads up to the security fence. There is a patch of worn grass behind the play house and a grassy area beside the portacabin. These two spaces are not in regular use. A corner of the grassy bank contains a spring, which makes this area very muddy at times.

Observation confirmed that this area was not accessible to the children. Plastic (adult-sized) garden chairs had been placed in a row to prevent the children going on the worn grass. Groups of children edged into this space however, and sat on the chairs to watch what was happening in the playing-field.

House

Close observation revealed the importance of the house as a social place. This was a wooden play structure donated by a local DIY store.

The house had a door and windows that looked out over the play surface and the decking. There was a plastic barbecue set, a table and chair in the house. Four children or more could squeeze inside. The house was in use most of the time. It was regularly used for group play and occasionally as an individual private space.

The children appeared to use the house for different purposes during the day. At times it was the focus for imaginative play. One episode involved children dancing in the house while they sang 'Bob the builder' and hammered, using toys that had been put out for use in another part of the outdoor space. After lunch the house became more of a 'time out' space for children to sit out of the way.

Timed observation provided a snapshot of the house's use during a 30-minute period in the morning (see Table 2.1).

Table 2.1: Use of the play house over a 30-minute period

Time	Children	Activity
10am	5	Sitting and hammering with tools and with their fists
10.15	1 plus 1	One boy by himself sawing at the window. Gets a chair to stand on so he can reach to saw above the window. A second child comes in to join him
10.30	0	A child comes to have a look in, sees it is empty and walks away

There was a large play house inside the preschool. Observation revealed this to be one of the most popular places inside. There were more opportunities for different games and for dressing up in the inside house.

Caterpillar

A large plastic caterpillar tunnel was regularly placed outside. The tunnel entrance was the stretched mouth of the caterpillar, which had protruding eyes. The tunnel was divided into sections. Each section was painted a different bright colour and was supported by circular feet in the same colours.

Observation showed this to be a physical space for children to demonstrate their climbing, balancing and jumping abilities. One game involved climbing on top of the caterpillar, jumping off onto the soft play surface, falling as if they had broken their arm, jumping up, giggling and starting again!

Logs

There were a few large, flat logs on the edge of the soft play surface. The children appeared to use these logs for balancing. One of the youngest children in the preschool took great pleasure in practising stepping from one log to another.

Compost tray lid

There was a plastic tray designed for holding water or sand. This piece of equipment came with a lid to keep the contents clean. The tray and lid were moulded into the shape of a car. The staff had filled the tray with compost and provided garden tools for the children to play with in the tray. During the observation the children did not show interest in the compost, however, but had adapted the lid as a seat. At one point, four girls and their dolls were sitting talking in the lid. Later in the session children built a bridge from the lid to the decking using boards and small bricks.

Inside sand pit

The observation was intended to focus on children's use of the outdoor space. However, due to rain, the children moved inside where the observation continued. This revealed the importance of the sand pit. The fixed sand pit takes up approximately a quarter of the floor space in one of the two rooms. The pit is filled with buckets, spoons, spades, cars and other sand toys. The children take their shoes off in order to go in the sand. It is an adult-free space.

This corner of the room is in constant use. Children use this space to dig and make up imaginative games. It also appears to be a space in which to relax, with children enjoying lying on their stomachs in the sand and talking to each other. Children can also stay outside, around the edge of the pit but still play with the sand. At one point during the observation four children were in the sand pit and eight were playing around the pit. This amounted to a third of the children present that morning engaged with the sand.

Looking through the fence

Close observation revealed the importance to the children of being able to watch what was happening outside the play area. The gaps in the security fence were wide enough for the children to see through. Twice during the observation period a group of children stopped to watch and comment on what was happening in the playing-field that surrounded the preschool. The first event was two older children bringing an Alsatian dog to play in the park. The second incident was the arrival of a man with a motorised lawnmower to cut the grass.

Figure 2.5: Excerpt from researcher's field notes

Child: Look, there are two boys. He's called Richard.

Child: What's the dog's name?

Child: Look, the dog is fetching the hoop.

Child: He might come right here.

[Five children are now standing and watching the older boys and the dog.]

The time spent observing the children provided an invaluable foundation for the rest of the project. The observations had identified a number of important places, including specific play equipment and popular activities outside. Place use included intended purposes, such as riding the bikes on the soft play surface, and inventive place use, such as sitting in the compost tray lid and spying through the fence.

We made a display of the photographs we had taken during the observation in the cloakroom area of the preschool. This display provided the opportunity for parents, practitioners and children to exchange thoughts about the outdoor space.

Next we provided a range of media and activities for the children to express their own views and experiences of the outdoor space using cameras, audiotape, book-making, tours, map-making and the Magic Carpet.

Cameras and book-making

Taking photographs

Photography proved a rewarding tool for finding out about young children's perspectives in the original project (Clark and Moss 2001). We had been surprised by the competency children demonstrated in using cameras and by the insights the photographs provided. These findings were echoed in the Spaces to Play project.

Fifteen children took part in this activity over a two-day period. Alison worked with the children in pairs or individually. Children were asked whether they would like to take photographs of the important things outside at the preschool. The phrase 'important things' emphasises our interest in which people, places and objects have meaning for the children.

We decided to experiment with two different types of camera, disposable cameras and basic reusable cameras. There were problems with the winding mechanisms of the cheap reusable cameras. The disposable cameras proved the most straightforward to use. Only one child in a pair had a camera at any time. This was important so that the researcher could listen and watch the children select and take their photographs.

A toy dog, Barney, was introduced by Alison at this stage of the project and continued through to the evaluation. We introduced this large floppy dog, kitted out in overalls and wellington boots to see if he encouraged the children to talk. Most children took to the idea of Barney as a visitor who, together with Alison the researcher, was here to find out about their outdoor space.

The children took to the photography activity with great interest. They moved purposefully around the outdoor space, going from one object or person to another in different areas of the garden. Some children chose to take ten or more photographs. One girl was unusual in that she took the whole film herself. One of the younger photographers (three years three months) started at the slide, moved around outside and then went inside to photograph important places there. Two children were too shy to take their own photographs but were happy to direct Alison to take a photograph of their chosen subject.

Children of different abilities were able to participate in this activity. The preschool has a number of children with speech and language delay and other special needs. Several of these children took great pleasure in using the camera. One boy was so keen to take his own photographs that he found it hard to wait to wind on the film. However, he mastered this skill and succeeded in taking his own photographs of places and people of his own choosing. When he had finished the film he handed the camera back to Alison and said: 'Thanks for that, mate.'

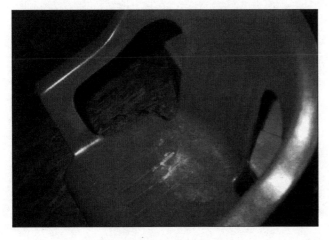

A close up of a chair in the play house by Ruth

Book-making using children's photographs

Children making books from their photographs had been introduced in the original study, almost as an afterthought, to provide children with their own record of taking part. However, the process of talking and listening to children as they selected their photographs and labelled their chosen images proved to be valuable so we gave time in the Spaces to Play project to build on this work.

We arranged for the children's photographs to be developed overnight and returned to the preschool to work with 10 of the children who had taken the most photographs. Two sets of photographs were made, one for the children and one for the research. Alison worked with a group of children, the children taking it in turns to look through their photographs. Barney the dog was part of this activity. The children were encouraged to tell Barney what each photograph was about.

The children expressed great pleasure in seeing their own photographs. They were delighted when they realised they had managed to capture their intended subjects, as one boy said: 'Got it!' This seemed to apply particularly when the photograph had been about an object of personal significance such as a model they had made.

Much discussion went on during the book-making. Some children liked to find a photograph and match it against the index card, which showed thumbnail pictures of each shot. Others asked to add their own captions to the photographs. Asking children to select the most important photographs provided another possible way of learning about their priorities.

Here are two descriptions of the books made by Alice and Jim, who were three years old.

Table 2.2: Description of photobook by Alice (age 3)

Alice's photobook	Child chosen caption	Subject matter
Cover	This is the gate	Close-up of gate to the playing-field
Page 1	This is N	Close-up of friend (boy)
Page 2	This is E	Close-up of friend (boy)
Page 3	Barney	Close-up of toy dog
Page 4	This is B and E	Close-up of two friends: a boy and a girl
Page 5	This is B and N	Close-up of two boys (one in full view)
Page 6	This is E	Close-up of friend (boy)
Page 7	This is N	Close-up of friend (girl)
Page 8	E and B again	Close-up of two friends: a boy and a girl

Alice was keen to include as many of her photographs as possible in her book. She chose a photograph of the gate in the perimeter fence as her cover. This was one of the two photographs not to feature any people. Seven of her remaining images were close-ups of friends, both girls and boys. The remaining image was of Barney the toy dog, which she had taken a particular 'shine' to.

Alice appeared to identify important places with the children she met there, rather than with toys or equipment.

Table 2.3: Description of photobook by Jim (age 3)

Jim's photobook	Child chosen caption	Subject matter
Cover	The train	Close-up of a train made out of construction toy
Page 1	A picture of the sky	Sky with clouds
Page 2	Another half of the train	Second close-up of train model
Page 3	The red carriage	Close-up of the red section of the caterpillar
Page 4	The green carriage	Close-up of the green section of the caterpillar
Page 5	The blue carriage	Close-up of the blue section of the caterpillar
Page 6	The train	Close-up of a train made out of construction toy

Jim was fascinated by trains. His photographs included the toy shed, clouds, the slide, several photographs of the caterpillar and his model of a train made using a construction toy. It was not until Jim sat down to talk about his photographs that the full extent of the personalised meanings he had given to the outdoor space became clear.

His photograph of the shed, which was the first photograph he had taken (and we thought had been a mistake), became a picture of the shed where the engines live. The caterpillar was not a brightly coloured insect but a string of carriages, which related to the colours of his favourite Thomas the Tank Engine characters.

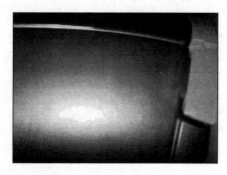

The 'blue carriage' taken by Jim

Table 2.4: A summary of themes from 60 children's photographs and book-making

Theme	Occurrences
Places associated with people	
children and adults	27
adults only	7
Large play equipment	
house (including inside shots)	12
caterpillar	10
climbing frame and slide	6
Natural features	8
Fence	19

What has been confirmed by the children using this tool?

Working with cameras and the book-making confirmed some general information about the place use and place preferences of children at the preschool. Places were chosen which included children and adults in almost half (27) of the 60 photographs selected for the books. However, it is perhaps surprising that adults were shown in only seven of the photographs. The adults included permanent staff, students and Alison, the researcher.

Several of these shots with adults in were about children and adults playing a board game or working on a picture together.

Three pieces of large play equipment featured in the books: the house (12 out of 60 photographs); the caterpillar (10 out of 60); and the climbing frame and slide (6 out of 60). This information confirmed the importance of the house and the caterpillar as two key play spaces.

Almost a third (19) of the photographs included shots of the perimeter fence. These included direct close-up shots of the fence together with other views that included the fence as background. The angle of the camera from the children's height confirmed the omnipresence of the fence. Their photographs made the outdoor space feel hemmed in and caged.

What new information has this given us?

Children's distinction between indoor and outdoor experiences was raised by one child's book. He chose two photographs of inside places for his book about the outside: the toilets and the indoor sand pit. This emphasised the importance of both these facilities in his life at the preschool, which an interview with his mother confirmed. He chose his photograph of the inside sand pit as the cover for his book. This supported the material gathered from other tools about the importance of the sand pit. It was a reminder that children do not necessarily place their indoor and outdoor experiences in 'separate boxes'.

Other photographs revealed small details of significance. For example, a general shot of the soft play surface was labelled by the photographer 'the ball', which was sitting in one corner of the picture. One child took a close-up shot of pebbles in a pram. However, there were few photographs selected of formal activities such as board games or jigsaws.

Children also revealed their interest in the weather and the natural environment. Several children chose photographs of the sky. Another showed the brightness of the sun shining against the fence.

In addition to this general information about the outdoor environment, children's photographs and books provided a glimpse of the individual 'landscapes' children established for themselves, as illustrated by Jim's book. These personal interpretations of the space would have remained hidden without the inclusion of this tool.

Tours

Child-led tours

We had found young children to be articulate guides of their immediate environment, both indoors and outdoors, in the original study (Clark and Moss 2001: 27–8). We were keen to include this as a multi-sensory way of tapping into young children's knowledge about their outdoor space at the preschool.

Two pairs of children took Alison around the outdoor space indicating the important places. The children were in charge of the route as well as how the tour was recorded. Each pair had a camera and carried a small tape recorder with a clip mike.

The tours took place on an overcast day when the outdoor space was not in use. Activities and equipment were not laid out but the large play equipment was still in place. This had an unexpected impact on the tours. When Alison asked the children about a particular space and what they liked to do there the children improvised and acted out their favourite activities. Two boys galloped around the play surface shouting, 'We're on the bikes.'

Figure 2.6: A summary of themes from the child-led tours

Important places

caterpillar: inside and out: *balancing, jumping, crawling, climbing*

house: inside and outside

scooter/purple bike

logs: *sitting and watching*

old bikes: *remembering*

spare ground – the show: *remembering*

decking: *building, playing games and colouring*

natural features – sky, earth, water in the tray: *exploring, sense of wonder*

shed: storing important things

What information has been confirmed by the children using this tool?

The importance of the house and caterpillar was reinforced by the photographs children took on the tour, and the use of the logs for sitting and watching, and the decking for building, colouring and playing games.

It was revealing that even when the bikes and scooters were not on show the children still demonstrated their significance, thus confirming information gathered in the observation and the use of cameras.

Small details were again shown to be important. One girl made a point of showing Alison the gravel pebbles between the soft play surface and the portacabin wall, and photographing them.

The wider environment was a feature of the tour. Children took photographs of the slope and the fence, and several photographs of the sky including a vapour trail. A beautiful leaf in a puddle on a chair was noticed and photographed.

A close up of a leaf by Colin and Robert

What new information has this given us?

Children revealed the importance of past events and memories. One boy took Alison to a space around the side of the portacabin. This tarmac surface was the possible site for a new room. Colin explained how this was where a show had happened: 'Sylvester and Tweety Pie'. Photographs were also taken of a pile of tangled bikes in a hidden corner beside the portacabin. These were no longer in use but were talked about affectionately.

Another piece of new information related to scale. Photographs taken inside the caterpillar tunnel revealed a cavernous hidden space ideal for crawling, sitting and talking. The photographs showed this to be a space where children could sit and watch the world.

■ Map-making

We found in the original study that children of three and four years old were able to engage in a map-making exercise when this was about an environment with which they were very familiar and had led a tour around (Clark and Moss 2001).

Eight children, including the four who had led the tours of the preschool site, made maps of the outdoor play space. The children used photos that they had taken, together with photocopies of photos by other children and Alison. Children added drawings to the maps to emphasise the important features.

These maps were made on large 'polos'. These were circular pieces of paper, approximately one metre across, with a hole in the middle. The aim was to enable children to think about the space 'in the round' and to be able to sit inside or outside of the circle in order to do so. The children included Barney the dog in this activity.

These maps were displayed in the cloakroom area, where parents, staff and children could discuss these perspectives on the outdoor space.

Close-up of a map made by
children after leading a tour

Practitioner and child
discuss a map together

Figure 2.7: Summary of themes from children's map-making

Photographs of:

play equipment: house, caterpillar, slide

people: adults, other children, themselves

natural features: pebbles, earth, leaf, sky

other features: the shed, logs, lid from the compost, fence and gate

toys: pram, old and new bikes, digger and bricks

Children's drawings of:

natural features: trees, apples

play equipment: inside the caterpillar

other features: a friend's T-shirt, patterns on the ground, the show

What information has been confirmed by the children using this tool?

The maps reinforced the importance of the key play features and the wider environment. The house, the caterpillar and the slide featured on the maps and were chosen by some of the children to be the first photos to put on the map.

One of the maps included three photos taken at different angles of the inside of the house; two of the furniture; and one showing two children.

Three of the four maps included photographs with adults with the children.

Some of the children chose photographs of their friends and one boy added a drawing of his friend's T-shirt.

The shed, the logs and the lid of the compost tray had all featured in earlier activities and children chose to include them on the maps. The fence and the gate were emphasised by close-up photographs on three of the four maps.

Children chose photos and added drawings of the natural world and the wider environment. These included detailed drawings of trees surrounding the play space, a leaf in a puddle on a chair, and several photos of clear and cloudy skies.

These details were matched by attention to the ground. Children photographed the earth and pebbles surrounding the edge of the soft play space. One group added 'the patterns on the ground'.

The sky taken by Jim and Ruth on their tour

The bikes featured in several ways: one group drew bikes on the map, another included a photograph of the favourite bikes in use, and two groups added a photograph of the tangled-up old bikes. Prams, buggies and push-along cars were chosen, together with smaller toys such as a ball and a digger.

What new information has this given us?

Children indicated the importance of including self-images on the maps. Children chose photographs of themselves taken by Alison and other children to ensure they were featured. This seems to emphasise how the space is connected to their feelings about themselves and their own identity.

Figure 2.8: Excerpt from map-making conversation

Child: Can I have me on there?

Alison: Oh, you. Yes, we'd better have you on the map. That's very important.

Child: (laughs) ... Because I like me.

The children who had led the tours found it easier to engage with the map-making process than the other children. This may be because the children who led the tours were more familiar with working with the researcher. It may, however, emphasise the importance of the children physically walking around a space and reflecting on its meanings before trying to represent that space in a two-dimensional way.

Making the maps is about talking to children and listening to them talk about their insights and their priorities. The verbal responses are as important as the visual information provided by the photographs and drawings, the meanings of which need to be discussed with the children.

Magic Carpet

Looking at and talking about slides

We added the 'Magic Carpet' as a new piece of the Mosaic approach for this pilot project. This was designed to open up new conversations with the children about their wider environment. What local spaces are children aware of, what is their experience of these places and what additional insights can this give to the current and future uses of their outdoor space? We made slide images of the local town centre, local landmarks and the park (all taken from a child's height). We added images of Alison's local park, as well as images taken during the project of the preschool's outdoor space. Students on placement in the preschool helped us convert the home corner inside the preschool into a darkened tent and the slides were shown to the children, while they sat on a 'Magic Carpet'.

This idea had been tried by Christine Parker (2001) after her trip to Reggio Emilia as a way of talking to young children about different places.

Children came into the tent to view the slides in small groups of four to six, with 28 children or more seeing the slides over a two-day period. Most children were keen to sit inside and watch the slides many times over, while others chose to peep in through the home corner windows. The darkened space and the slide projector provided opportunities for playing with shadows as well as engaging with the images on show.

Figure 2.9: Summary of themes from the Magic Carpet activity

Children shared the following experiences following watching the slides:

going shopping

sitting on the sculpture seat with their parents and sharing sweets

walking their dog

climbing the slopes

rolling on the grass

going on their bikes

sitting on the tree stumps

feeding the ducks

riding in the boats

seeing squirrels looking for nuts

other parks they had been to: 'Its got lots of things: a little slide, a big slide, and roundabouts and a see-saw.'

What information had been confirmed by using this tool?

Children's conversations about the slides confirmed the pleasure they took in exploring their environment. This included references to riding their bikes along the paths of the park, climbing the slopes and references to the animals and plants.

What new information had been gained by including this tool?

We gained some insight into children's knowledge of their wider environment through using the slides. This included comments about the built environment as well as the natural features. The most animated conversations were held about a slide of the 'Millennium seat'. This seat had been designed by a sculptor and was situated in a pedestrianised area beside a popular store on the high street. Children talked about sitting on the seat with their families and eating sweets on a Saturday.

Slides of Alison's local park provoked comparisons with the children's favourite parks and descriptions of the play equipment there. It would have been good to extend this activity by the children taking the researcher on a tour of the town and their favourite parks. However, the slides provided an alternative way of bringing children's knowledge about other spaces into conversations about their outdoor play space.

We have described in the Introduction that the Mosaic approach combines traditional with participatory methods. This next section outlines how we adapted interviews, a traditional research tool, to gather young children's perspectives and those of practitioners and parents.

■ Child interviews

Talking about preferences and priorities

Twenty children were interviewed in order to offer the opportunity for more formal conversations about how children used the outdoor space and so that they could talk about their feelings about different aspects of the space. The questions were structured but the format of the interviews remained flexible. Where possible these were conducted outside in a place where the children appeared relaxed. Some of the interviews were conducted in the play house, or walking around.

The questions were adapted from the original study by the researcher, with the help of colleagues from Learning through Landscapes. The questions began by using Barney, the toy dog, as the focus:

- If Barney wanted to hide outside at [the preschool] where could he go?
- If Barney wanted to sit and talk to a friend outside at [the preschool] where could he go?
- If Barney wanted to run and climb what could he do outside?
- If Barney wanted to be with a grown-up outside what could he do?

These initial questions were designed to see if children linked emotions and activities with certain locations. Further questions asked about what they liked and didn't like about their preschool, and where were their favourite places inside and outside. Specific questions were added to the schedule about the house and the fence as a result of children's responses to the other tools (see Appendix A).

We interviewed the children in a variety of ways: in small friendship groups of three, in pairs on the move outside or individually. The arrangements were deliberately kept flexible in order to include the views of as many children as possible. Some of the shyer children were happy to be interviewed as part of a group but would have been reluctant to answer questions in a one-to-one situation. Some of the more articulate children were happy to talk and were less likely to dominate other children's answers if they were interviewed by themselves.

Figure 2.10: Example from child interview

If Barney wanted to hide outside at [the preschool] where could he go?
Henry and Bob: Round the side.

If Barney wanted to sit and talk to a friend outside at [the preschool] where could he go?
Henry and Bob: On the table. You don't sit on the floor.

If Barney wanted to run and climb what could he do outside?
Bob and Henry: Round here [soft play area].

If Barney wanted to be with a grown-up outside what could he do?
Henry and Bob: Inside there.

Tell Barney about the house.
Henry: This is where we play and talk and cook …
Bob: … and sit on the chair.
Henry: And I can whistle.

Tell Barney about the fence.
Bob: [It's] to keep the dogs out …
Henry: … and to keep the naughty people out, the strangers.

What do you like about [the preschool]?
Henry: The cars and the sand pit and outside, yeah, and playing on the cars and the bikes and scooters and the inside sand pit.

What don't you like about being here?
Henry: I like everything I don't like nothing.
Bob: I don't like [x: child's name] (Henry agreed).

Where is your favourite place inside?
Henry: In the sand pit.
Bob: When you sit and listen to story time and when me and Henry standed together sometime.

Where is your favourite place outside?
Henry: In this car – all the cars.
Bob: Playing on the scooters, cars and the bikes.

Where don't you like outside?
Henry: I don't like playing over there [the decking].

What would you like to do more often outside at [the preschool]?
Henry: On the bikes and scooters and cars and stuff.
Bob: Play.

What is missing outside at [the preschool]?
Henry: We have a slide but we haven't got a swimming pool.

What do you think should happen on the grassy parts of [the preschool]?
Henry: I like it here [looking at the muddy bit].

Is there anything else Barney needs to know about [the preschool]?
Henry and Bob: shake heads

(Full transcript of child interviews with two friends, aged 4)

Figure 2.11: Summary of themes from the child interviews

What were the favourite places outside?

Playing in the house

Riding on the bikes, cars and scooters

Rolling in the mud

Playing with the toy animals, toy cars and magnet trains

Being with favourite people – adults and children

What would children like to do more often outside?

Play

Play on the cars, bikes and scooters

Go on the see-saw

Stamp up and down

Play in the caterpillar

Make drawings

Cutting

'Play at my house'

What information had been confirmed by using this tool?

The interviews provided the opportunity to ask the children directly about their experiences and preferences about the outdoor space. Their responses reinforced the importance of the soft play area for the bikes, cars and scooters and the value children placed on the house and the caterpillar.

Eleven of the 14 children (who responded to the question about what they liked about their preschool) specifically mentioned an outdoor activity. This confirmed our general impression about the overall importance of the outdoor space for the children.

What new information had been gained by including this tool?

Imaginative play

Children's responses provided another layer of detail to the material gathered using the other tools. New insight about the use of the house was one such example. Answering the question, 'Tell Barney about the house', children were quick to describe the imaginative games they played there:

> This is where we play and talk and cook. (Henry, see above)
> We play doctors, we play vets. See this? You put the chair there and you lie down on it. (Julie)
> When it's night time it gets dark. Bats are hanging on the window sills. I love staying there, all there. (Jim)

Their responses appeared to be more detailed when we asked the question whilst sitting in the house. Less articulate children were also able to contribute. For example, Martin who had speech and language delay did not reply to the question directly, but launched into a role-play game with Alison: 'Water comes in the house ... we better run ... let's go.'

Access

The interviews provided new information about children's understandings of access. Their responses to the question: 'Tell Barney about the fence' highlighted how the perimeter fence was understood as a barrier to keep others out:

> To keep the dogs out. (Bob)
> ... and to keep the naughty people out, the strangers. (Henry)

Interestingly, the open space owned by the local authority which surrounded the preschool was not seen as a child-friendly place:

> You are not allowed to go past there. That's the dog park.
> The dog park is up there. (Ruth)

Children's responses to this question indicated that they also associated the word fence with the portable barriers used by the preschool to stop children going on certain areas. These barriers had cartoon people painted on them.

> ... because we don't go down there. (Lee)
> We're not allowed over there. (Petra)
> That's about so when it's wet on the grass or wet on the caterpillar you shouldn't go there. (Julie)

Future changes

The interview responses gave us some indication of what activities children would like to do more often outside. This is an example of information that needed a direct question in order to emerge. The push-and-ride toys were the most popular. Children were very specific about the hierarchy of these toys. Several children were insistent about their particular preference:

> Not the bikes, cars. I like playing. (Martin)
> Riding on the scooters and the bikes. First scooter. Then bike. (Jim)

Creative activities were mentioned alongside the push-and-rides:

> I'd like to do drawings and cutting. I like the bikes. (Alice, Kim and Louise)

Children mentioned access to play equipment that wasn't in frequent use:

> On the see-saw. (Ester)

Above all, children wanted to have more opportunities to play:

> Playing out there [on the soft play area]. (Milly, Alice and Bill)
> Play. (Bob)
> Like playing. Stamping up and down on the soft things. I like playing with the horses and stuff. (Julie)

A less helpful question was 'What is missing outside at [your preschool]?'

Our intention was to tap into children's experiences of other play spaces and play experiences at home, so they might mention activities or equipment they thought they would like at their preschool. Jim's response was the kind of answer we had expected:

> Another bike because the tangled-up bikes are missing. We took a picture of them.

However, other children made a more literal interpretation of the word 'missing':

> The windows. (Mollie, Alice and Bob)

These children were interviewed in the house where vandals had thrown a stone and cracked one of the windows, which had since been removed.

Children's responses to the interviews reinforced the importance of including this opportunity for talking and listening within the Mosaic approach. We followed these interviews with short interviews with practitioners and parents.

Practitioner interviews

We carried out short individual interviews with the manager and three of her staff (see Appendix B). The practitioners were chosen to represent those with over 10 years' experience at the preschool and those who had recently joined. There were several reasons for including these interviews. First, we felt it to be very important to involve practitioners in this process of listening, rather than to sideline their views. The interview provided a formal opportunity to acknowledge that their opinions were valid and their knowledge about the children was valuable. Second, we were interested in gathering their perspectives about children's use of the outdoor space and, third, to hear about their ideas for change.

Figure 2.12: Excerpt from practitioner interview

Where do you think are the children's favourite places outside?

In the house and they like playing on the decking – if there are supervised activities they like that.

And on the caterpillar when the grass is not too muddy.

They love it … and like to stand on it!

Where do you think they don't like?

Don't think there is anywhere. The hill bit. It's dangerous. They are not allowed on it.

Where might they go to hide?

Playing games in the house and places they are not allowed behind the shed, not many places to hide, the shed, under the caterpillar.

Where might they go to sit and talk to their friends?

Decking, in the house, the safety surface.

Where might they go to run and climb?

Grass, caterpillar, safety surface – but not if all the toys are out.

What do you enjoy doing with the children outside?

I enjoy everything – like playing games with them. Puzzles. Taking out drawing.

What information had been confirmed by using this tool?

The practitioners identified the house, the bikes and caterpillar as children's favourite places outside. They identified similar places to the children as places to hide, to sit and talk and to run and climb.

They identified the fence as an area that needed change. Practitioners acknowledged that the children's photographs had led to this awareness.

What new information had been gained by including this tool?

Interviewing the practitioners highlighted differences of opinion between the children and the adults. The house provoked the most striking contrast of comments. We had heard from the children, and observed from their play, how important the house was. The practitioners were aware of how popular the house was but they had reservations about its current use:

> Children use the house, they tend to use it as a buffer. Some think it's a wonderful activity in there … then it can become a fight … [they] lob things out of the window or shout. But I don't think it's used successfully, even if three [children are there]. They like taking toys in but … the main problem is, it's too small. (Heather)

> The house originally faced the shed. It was absolutely hopeless. They belted from one side to the other so we moved it round so it is part of the quiet area. It's all right for two children but it isn't big enough to put things in. We are trying to make use of it … I wish it was twice as large (some kids smashed the window). (Louise)

Problems with the house for the adults revolved around its size compared with the number of children now using the preschool, and the children's use of the space. It was acknowledged that the house was sometimes used as a buffer zone for children to retire to for time out from adults. However, most of the time the activities were felt to be too noisy and disruptive, and needed constant supervision.

Interviewing the practitioners helped us to clarify their views on what changes could be made. A space to dig was one new feature discussed:

> A digging area come building site that doesn't need us to say constantly 'get out of there'. I'd like them just to dig. (Heather)

Water play was another activity that the children hadn't discussed but which would add another dimension to the outdoor play space.

◼ Parent interviews

Parents' perspectives on their children's priorities and interests can add another layer of detail to this approach. We selected four parents to interview. These parents (all mothers) were not chosen as a representative sample but all had children involved in the research who had used several of the tools and were themselves knowledgeable about the outdoor space at the preschool.

The questions were designed to draw on parents' understandings of what their children enjoyed doing inside and outside at home and at preschool (see Appendix C).

We interviewed the parents towards the end of the fieldwork, after they had seen their children's photobooks.

Figure 2.13: Excerpt from parent interview

What do you think would be a good day for your daughter at the preschool?

If painting is involved. Keyworking. The one-to-one.

She likes the caterpillar outside. She enjoys structure – knowing the rules.

The sand pit.

What do you think would be a bad day for her at the preschool?

If no one had paid her close attention.

Probably a day when she'd not gone outside.

One when spent drawing.

Do you think she enjoys being outside at [the preschool]?

Yes she does. It adds a sense of security because it's safe – no strangers.

What do you think she enjoys doing outside here?

The play house – [or inside] role-play is a key thing here. The caterpillar.

What information had been confirmed by using this tool?

The parent interviews, although a small sample, confirmed the importance of the outdoor space to the children. Parents identified the house, the caterpillar and the bikes as favourite activities. One parent explained:

> Likes going on the bikes. Crashing. He doesn't ride bikes much at home. He does his indoor activities outside so if the sand tray was outside he would be there.

This comment explains how children's favourite activities at preschool may not necessarily duplicate activities at home but be those things which they do not have the opportunity to do elsewhere. Interestingly, several parents highlighted the importance of the sand pit and raised the possibility of more opportunities for digging outside.

What new information had been gained by including this tool?

Speaking to individual parents helped to increase our knowledge about each of their children's preferences. Some of this information was relevant to their child only, whereas other material highlighted possibilities for improving the space for all the children.

One parent, for example, described how her son had a shed at home where he loved to sit and had put pictures of trains on the wall. This furthered our understanding of the picture we had been building up of her son, using the other tools. It accentuated the difference between children sharing a small house at preschool with five other children and being in control of a similar sized space at home to retreat to.

A more general observation from the parents was how their children enjoyed helping with tasks in the garden such as weeding, planting seeds and feeding the birds.

The parents offered some interesting possibilities for how the outdoor space could be improved. The parents, like the practitioners, had been made to think in a new way about the facilities because of the children's photographs:

> Got it into my head about the fence. Use the bank and could spy out. The bank as a high spot, for example with binoculars, like in a nearby park. More tunnels and natural things.

This idea about making the bank into a feature supported the use the children already made of spying through the fence. We raised this suggestion with practitioners during the next stage of the project, the review.

Each of these children had access to a garden at home. It would be important in a further study to interview parents whose children only had access to public spaces.

Stage Two

Reviews

Stage One of the pilot project focused on gathering material. Stage Two involved children and adults reviewing the material, discussing meanings and reflecting on what were the important places and uses of space. We held reviews with the children, practitioners and with Learning through Landscapes.

Although we describe the gathering and reviewing as two distinct phases, in reality these stages become to some extent blurred. For example, practitioners began to review the children's use of the outdoor space when we placed photographs from the observation in the cloakroom area during the first weeks of the project. Reflecting on meanings and reassessing understandings took place throughout the whole project, but this second stage allows a concentrated period of reflection.

We wanted to make the review as focused as possible on the children's perspectives. We made a book of the children's comments and photographs to centre the review on the children. This was designed in story form, with Barney the dog as the main character together with a cartoon caterpillar. We read the book to the children during two morning sessions. The children sat with Barney while the story was read and they were encouraged to add their comments to the text.

Following these sessions with the children we used the book as a prompt for reviewing the material with practitioners during two staff meetings. The idea of these sessions was to present the information gathered from the children, parents and the practitioners themselves for discussion. Priorities for change were discussed and areas for continuity highlighted.

Review with the children

The children appeared to enjoy listening to their comments and seeing their photographs. They were keen to point out their own contributions to the book. However, the question in the book about what should happen to the unused part of the garden did not lead to many comments. Children described this part of the garden as where they were not allowed to go. This response indicated to us the importance of allowing children access to a new space in order to give them 'permission' to explore new possibilities.

A review with Alison, two children and Barney, the toy dog

Review with practitioners

The review began with practitioners reflecting on their impressions of the project. They discussed their surprise at the abilities the children demonstrated with the cameras. The manager described how the project had led her team to change their ways of working with the children. The children's competency had given the adults the confidence to rely less on planning ahead and to place more emphasis on following child-led projects.

The following issues were highlighted as priorities for change in the outdoor space:

■ overcrowding in the house
■ access to the slope and minimising the negative impact of the fence.

Both of these issues will be discussed in detail in Stage Three.

Review with Learning through Landscapes

Alison and the Early Years Development Officer from Learning through Landscapes met to review the material from the children, parents and practitioners. It was important here to bring together the visual and verbal evidence. Each of the tools was discussed in turn in order to reveal emerging themes. Discussions centred around two main questions:

■ Where do children see as the important places in this outdoor space?
■ How do the children use these places?

Summaries of these themes from each tool were mapped out on a large plan. Similar ideas were linked and conflicting meanings noted. This led to Stage Three: deciding areas of continuity and change.

Stage Three

We identified four categories of places in the outdoor space, following the gathering and reviewing of the material:

- places to keep
- places to expand
- places to change
- places to add.

This next section illustrates examples of each of these categories and demonstrates which tools were helpful in reaching these decisions.

Places to keep: the caterpillar

It had been apparent from our first visit that the children enjoyed this strange shape. However, the use of the different research tools had emphasised just how important this piece of equipment was for the children. The multiple uses, both shared and private, emerged from using this combination of tools. This was a space to climb over, balance on, rest on top of and hide inside. This was a play space not to try to change.

Inside the caterpillar taken by
Colin and Robert

Table 2.5: Places to keep: the caterpillar

Research tool	Information gathered about the caterpillar
Observation	Children used the caterpillar as a social place and a physical space. They enjoyed balancing on top of the shape, jumping off and pretending to hurt themselves!
Cameras and book-making	The caterpillar was in 10 of the 60 photographs taken by the children and chosen for inclusion in their books. These included inside and outside shots of the caterpillar. This was a place in which to hide, talk to friends and watch what was happening outside. The use of cameras revealed personal meanings for the caterpillar. One child who was fascinated by trains took photographs of each section of the caterpillar and called them 'carriages'.
Tours and map-making	Children took photographs inside and outside on their tours and included these photographs on their maps, reinforced by a drawing of the caterpillar.
Practitioner interviews	One practitioner identified inside the caterpillar as one of the children's favourite places outside 'because there aren't other places to hide'. Another wasn't sure whether the children liked it or not: 'I wonder if they don't like the caterpillar? They'd probably like it.'
Child interviews	Children identified the caterpillar as a place to sit and talk to a friend: 'on the caterpillar and under the caterpillar'. One child described playing in the caterpillar as the activity he would like to do more often at the preschool.

Places to expand: the house

This play space had been donated to the preschool by a local DIY store. Observing the children revealed this to be a key resource for the children. The children confirmed this through their photographs, the tour and their interviews. Parents mentioned the house as an important space in the preschool, and talked about similar play spaces at home. However the interviews with practitioners showed that the house was a source of tension. The house was felt to be too small for the numbers of children using the outdoor space. This multi-method approach had made these differences visible.

The review with children, practitioners and Learning through Landscapes recognised these opposing views and discussed possibilities that would acknowledge the value of the imaginative play in new ways.

Table 2.6: Places to expand: the house

Research tool	House
Observation	Children used the house as a social place. It is a space for being noisy, talking together and for imaginative play.
Cameras and book-making	The house was in 12 of the 60 photographs taken by the children and chosen for inclusion in their books. These included inside and outside shots. This was a place in which to hide, talk to friends and watch what was happening outside.
Tours and map-making	Children took photographs inside and outside on their tours and included these photographs on their maps.
Practitioners' interviews	Practitioners recognised the children used the house for multiple purposes: They tend to use it as a buffer … it can be a bun fight … they lob things out of the window or shout. Three out of the four practitioners interviewed named the house as the item they would like to give away.
Parents' interviews	One parent identified the house as somewhere she thought her child enjoyed playing outside at the preschool: 'Role play is a key thing here.' Another parent described how her child had a play house at home: 'He loves his little house. He puts pictures up in his house of trains.'
Child interviews	The children gave detailed descriptions of what happens in the house, for example: 'We play doctors, we play vets, see this – you put the chair there and you lay down on it'; 'This is where we play and talk and cook'; 'It's got a table and chairs and a roof. Hide and seek because you can hide under the table. You bump your head.' Several identified the house as their favourite place while others recognised that it could get too noisy: 'I don't like playing doggies in here – it's too noisy, too many in here, some of the teachers gets one of them out.'

■ Places to change: the fence

From a visitor's point of view, the security fence was a noticeable feature of the outdoor space. However, the children's photographs and maps emphasised how domineering this feature was. Close observation revealed another dimension. The gaps in the security fence were wide enough for the children to see through. Twice during the observation period a group of children stopped to watch and comment on what was happening in the playing-field that surrounded the preschool. Any solution needed to bear in mind the importance of leaving spaces for the children to see through – so the people-spotting and dog-watching could continue. Ideas discussed included adding temporary weaving to the fence, placing paint boards on the fence and having binoculars and telescopes available for long-distance viewing.

The fence taken by Alice

Table 2.7: Places to change – the fence

Research tool	Fence
Observation	Children enjoyed spying things happening, through the fence.
Cameras and book-making	The fence was shown in almost two-thirds of the photographs taken by the children and selected for their books. These included images of the lawnmower in the playing-field and close-up images of the fence in the sunlight. Their photographs made the outdoor space feel hemmed in and caged.
Tours and map-making	Children included photographs of the fence on their maps.
Practitioners' interviews	Practitioners described surprise about what the fence looked like from the children's perspective in their photographs.
Child interviews	Children demonstrated their awareness of why the fence was necessary: 'to keep the naughty people, the strangers out'; 'you are not allowed to go past there. That's the dog park. The dogs' park is up there.'

Places to add: new seating and digging

The research process identified places that could be added to the outdoor space to maximise the children's enjoyment. The first of these was more places for adults and children to sit together. The observation showed adults sitting with children on the decking, which children confirmed in their interviews. There was a lack of other places for this to happen. The 'Magic Carpet' slide-show drew on children's wider knowledge of places where they liked to sit. One such place was the Millennium seat in the local town, designed by an artist.

One possibility discussed was to add seating for adults and children to sit comfortably together around the play space.

Table 2.8: Places to add – shared seating

Research tool	Seating
Observation	The decking area at times provided a quieter space where children could go if they wanted to be with an adult.
Cameras and book-making	Adults were shown in seven of the 60 photographs taken by the children and chosen for their books. These included photographs of adults and children sitting together and playing a board game or working on a picture together.
Tours and map-making	Children pointed out stacked plastic chairs with a puddle and a leaf but these were used as a barrier to keep children away from certain areas.
Practitioners' interviews	One practitioner pointed out that the children liked to sit on the adult chairs if they were available. Three of the four practitioners interviewed described sitting on the decking and chatting with the children or playing board games as one of the things they enjoyed doing most outside.
Child interviews	Children were asked 'If Barney wanted to be with a grown-up outside what could he do?' They didn't mention sitting together but identified the climbing frame as a piece of play equipment that always had an adult near it.
Magic Carpet	Children talked about sitting on the Millennium seat with their parents and sharing sweets from Woolworths, and sitting on tree stumps in Tonbridge Castle grounds.

The second gap identified was places to dig. The inside sand pit was a significant feature of the preschool. Observation had shown how popular this was as a relaxing space where children could take their shoes off and climb in. We have already noted the child who put a photograph of the inside sand pit on the cover in his book of important outdoor spaces! The opportunities to dig outside in the compost tray were not taken up by the children. However, parents talked about how their children liked to dig outside. Practitioners discussed adding a digging area as a new feature of the outdoor space.

Table 2.9: Places to add – outdoor sand pit

Research tool	Digging
Observation	The indoor sand pit was very popular. However, the outdoor compost tray remained untouched. Children used the lid of the tray for imaginative play instead.
Cameras and book-making	One child included a photograph of the indoor sand tray in his book.
Tours and map-making	Close-up photographs of the mud were included on the maps and drawings added.
Practitioners' interviews	Practitioners' ideas included seeing the children planting a vegetable patch or flowers and introducing a messy area for digging.
Parents' interviews	One parent mentioned introducing sand outside as a possible change: 'Sand outside is nice … and they associate it with the beach', and all four parents interviewed talked about the children enjoying digging and growing flowers.
Child interviews	Some children talked about the sand pit as their favourite place inside.

The indoor sand pit taken by James

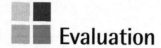

Evaluation

This has been the first time that we have used the Mosaic approach in an outdoor context. We thought it important to carry out an evaluation of this process. The following views were gathered in this 'stakeholder' evaluation:

1. The manager of the preschool and practitioners. A short questionnaire was handed out after the final session. These were filled in by the early years staff in their own time.

2. Children. A participatory activity was arranged at the end of the project to gather children's views about taking part. A large chart was made with windows for each of the tools the children had used. Behind each window were photographs to illustrate the activities the children had taken part in. Children met with Alison outside in small groups to talk about the chart.

3. Learning through Landscapes representative. A short questionnaire was sent by email.

Unfortunately, there was not enough time for parents' views to be formally included, although the manager and practitioners referred anecdotally to the positive reaction of the parents.

Manager and practitioners

The approach

The manager and the two practitioners who took part in the evaluation were surprised at how competent children of different abilities had shown themselves to be with a camera:

> What the children achieved with the cameras was a great surprise to me. Even some children who would seem 'less able' were able to contribute. *(Manager)*

The cameras and the talking that they inspired were seen as the tool that worked best with the children:

> I particularly liked the way the children talked to you about their photos, and what they liked about the garden.
> *(Practitioner)*

The following positive elements of the project were also mentioned:

- wall maps: '... were great fun – enjoyed by all the children and parents – not just those who took part' (Manager)
- close observation of the children
- ongoing nature of the project over several weeks.

The Magic Carpet slide-show was the one element identified as not working so well, due to the numbers of children who wanted to take part at the same time. This pressure could be avoided if the slide-show was introduced over a longer period, enabling the activity to be less of a novelty and ensuring that each child could participate.

Outdoor space

The manager and practitioners described the following messages they had learned from the project about children's use of the outdoor space and possibilities for change:

- the children enjoy all aspects of the outdoor space and use all the areas
- the children enjoy the play house – even though practitioners generally find it unsuccessful
- the need to make the fence more friendlier
- the need for more places to be quiet and private
- the need to reconsider the use of the empty ground as children see it as an area they are not allowed to play in.

Children

There were two reasons for involving children in the evaluation. First, this provided an opportunity to say thank you to the children for taking part in the pilot project. Each child was given a thank you sticker from Barney. Second, it was in keeping with the participatory nature of the project to include the children's perspectives about the process.

Children sat in groups outside on the decking and talked about the photographs behind each of the windows on the chart. They were then asked to put a star sticker on the activity they had enjoyed taking part in most of all. The photographs chosen by the children included:

- inside the caterpillar
- Barney the dog
- one of the boys taking a photograph
- a girl wearing a friend's mask.

It seemed however that the children were commenting on which photograph they liked best rather than on the adults' own view of the exercise: which activity did you like doing best?

In practice the young age of the children in this project made it difficult to gather their views in this way. The main problem was the gap in time between the children's main involvement in the project, which ended in December, and the evaluation, which took place in early February.

However, while the children were taking part in the individual activities during the autumn, they had demonstrated their enthusiasm for the project, for example using toy cameras in their role-play and persistently asking to take part. There was one child whose enthusiasm was translated into a desire to write for the first time at the preschool. He wrote captions in his own 'writing' to each of his photographs.

This impression of their enjoyment was supported by the practitioners' views: 'They thoroughly enjoyed it'; 'All the children who took part enjoyed it'.

Learning through Landscapes

The approach

The Early Years Development Officer from Learning through Landscapes commented on the benefit of the multi-method approach for the children and other user groups:

> One strength is that the picture is built up over time and from many contributions of information from a variety of sources. It ensures that the picture that emerges reflects the needs and interests of the many rather than the few.

> Because details and ideas were revisited through several techniques – that is, the photos taken by children were made into books and discussed with the original child as well as with a wider audience – children had a chance to reflect and elaborate upon their ideas.

The role of a researcher as outsider was seen to have both a positive and negative effect.

> A further positive spin-off of the project is the chance for staff to see children's responses – staff were sometimes surprised at children's level of engagement, achievement and enthusiasm for the activities with Alison, for example, the child who 'wrote' in his book.

Practitioners were able to see children in a different light and their assumptions were challenged. However, the outsider role did mean that at times there was a mismatch of interests between the preschool's agenda for the day and the needs of the research.

> I think the weakness of the approach is that it is delivered by an 'outsider' to the group. This resulted in some 'conflicts of interest' between the permanent staff and the researcher re children's activities, for example, Christmas concert preparations going on around some important discussions with children re their outdoor space. Or an activity [tours] having to take place outdoors at a time when no equipment was out. However, all credit is due to Alison that she managed to overcome these difficulties.

The outdoor space

It was important to establish whether this pilot project had been a support or a hindrance to Learning through Landscape's work in supporting change to the outdoor space.

> The researcher's work with the children, parents and staff at the preschool has clarified what the important issues are for each user group. This has had a positive impact on my work with the preschool since it will allow me to pick up the threads and continue the process to the next stage – implementing the changes.

This evaluation marked the official end of the six-month pilot project. However, the important final steps of the project were carried out by the preschool in consultation with Learning through Landscapes.

■ Changes into practice: physical changes

Following the completion of the research project, the manager and the Early Years Development Officer from Learning through Landscapes met to draw up an action plan to inform the ongoing development of the space. The plan was based on the aims described in Figure 2.14.

Figure 2.14: Action plan drawn up by the preschool following the research

> *Developing children's use of the whole garden*
>
> Aims:
>
> ■ to work towards children having free-flow access to outdoors
>
> ■ to develop the use of the remaining part of the garden, incorporating ideas from children, staff, parents, committee
>
> ■ to address issues raised through the research with children in existing part of garden
>
> ■ to improve the staff's confidence, motivation and enthusiasm for supporting children's learning outdoors
>
> ■ to continue to develop the curriculum outdoors.

Through Learning through Landscapes, the preschool was able to benefit from a Team Challenge organised by an energy company. A group from the company gave a day of their time to remove a hazardous area of concrete from the outdoor space, which had remained an unused part of the garden.

Changes to the outdoor space have been led by two parents, Juliet Kelly and Alison Douch, whose commitment, hard work and imagination have transformed the space. The parents have listened to the children's accounts about their existing space. The changes have included:

■ a large outdoor sand pit
■ seats for adults and children to sit together
■ large plywood paint boards and chalk boards in the shapes of butterflies and caterpillars attached to the fence
■ hiding posts by the fence to spy around
■ turfed area for imaginative play using temporary resources.

The sensory garden includes tiny features such as glass nuggets set into cement circles in a camomile lawn. These reflect attention to the kind of detail that children included in their photographs and maps.

Changes to the outdoor space
(Photo taken by Juliet Kelly)

■ Changes into practice: attitudes, routines and planning

This project focused on changes to the outdoor environment. However, its impact has been wider than the physical changes to the outdoor space. Practitioners reported a change in attitude towards the children, acknowledging unexpected capabilities and interests. This has led to changes in planning and to routines.

> There is a tendency in nursery education to plan each week as a separate part of the curriculum. This term we have introduced themes which will hopefully be developed by the children, rather than being adult-directed.
> *(Manager)*

The manager has had the confidence to allow the children to take more of a lead in developing their thinking and learning.

Perhaps most encouraging of all is to see a preschool that now has the confidence to introduce open access to the outdoors. The children demonstrated through the research how important the outdoor environment was to their lives in the preschool. The practitioners and parents have listened to the children and, with the support of external help, have brought about change to their everyday routines.

Part Three:

Messages for Research and Practice

We will move in this final section from the specific case study to look at the general issues raised by using the Mosaic approach with young children. This will include three key elements:

- messages for practitioners using the Mosaic approach to make changes to the outdoor environment
- messages for practitioners linking the Mosaic approach and learning
- messages for researchers using the Mosaic approach with young children.

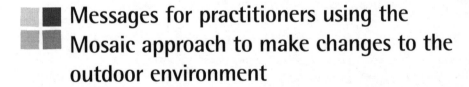

Messages for practitioners using the Mosaic approach to make changes to the outdoor environment

Our starting point for the Spaces to Play project followed the advice from the Carnegie Young People's Initiative to 'start early and to start locally' when beginning to involve children in decision-making. This led us to choose an institutional outdoor space as the arena for the project: an immediate environment with which young children were well acquainted.

As we have described in Part Two, the children were able to demonstrate detailed knowledge of their outdoor space, which included personal landmarks and shared places. This provided the practitioners, parents and researchers with visible evidence of the children's interests and preferences. This platform of knowledge provided the basis for change.

How could practitioners adapt the Mosaic approach for listening about outdoor spaces? The following section explores practical issues – each topic begins with questions to use as a starting point for discussion.

 Aim high

Starting points

■ What expectations do you have for young children's abilities to reflect on their outdoor environment?

■ Which children do you have lower expectations about and how could you support their involvement?

The Mosaic approach starts from the premise that gathering young children's perspectives is an essential part of working with young children, and not an added extra. A set of expectations comes with using this approach. Practitioners need to expect that:

■ young children are knowledgeable about their environment
■ young children have important insights to give
■ young children can express their views and experiences if the right tools and time are provided.

Some children will require more careful 'tuning in' to their preferred ways of communicating than others.

◼ Providing the tools and the time

Starting points

■ How could the Mosaic approach build on your current use of cameras and digital technology?

■ How could time and space for reviewing the children's material be arranged?

The Mosaic approach relies on children being given the time and the opportunity to express themselves in different ways. This acknowledges the 'hundred languages' (Edwards and others 1998) that children may use to explore their experiences. This may lead practitioners to introduce a new tool or build on existing tools in use in the early years setting.

Cameras are one example of a tool that our research suggests young children may find helpful. The preschool where the Spaces to Play project took place did not have an established tradition of adults or children using cameras to document everyday activities. In this context, children were introduced to cameras for the first time in an early years context. However, many came with their own home knowledge of older siblings or other members of their families taking photographs. Children in other early years institutions may be used to having access to cameras, including digital cameras and video cameras. There are many possibilities for using this developing technology to empower young children to express their views. One possibility would be for children to use a videocamera to record the tour of the site.

Whatever tools are chosen, it is important for practitioners to feel confident in supporting children in the use of these different media and to allow the children to take the lead. There is a time implication if children are to become familiar with new technology. However the process of acquiring new skills and interacting with the environment in a different way is as valuable as any more formal outcomes, such as books or maps produced (see 'Messages for practitioners linking the Mosaic approach and learning', pages 81 to 96).

However, the Mosaic approach is more than giving children tools in isolation to experiment with. The tools are a bridge for adults and children to review perspectives together, to discuss and negotiate meanings. This reviewing takes time. But at every stage new insights can be gained by discussing with children their meanings – whether through their photographs, the maps or recordings of their interviews.

■ Opportunities for stretching children's horizons

Starting points

■ How could you find out about children's knowledge of their local area?

■ What role might parents or older siblings play in identifying favourite family places?

There is a difficulty in involving children of whatever age in design projects if their present experiences of engaging places and spaces has been limited. This may be especially so where changes are being considered to an outdoor area that is at present a tarmac square or a muddy patch. There appear to be two considerations here: how can practitioners tap into children's knowledge of other positive places and experiences; and, second, how can practitioners introduce children to new possibilities?

We explored one way of approaching both these questions through the Magic Carpet idea: showing children slides of their wider environment and other play spaces. Slides and other visual images, however, keep children one step removed from play environments. Watching slides of different play spaces is second-best to being able to explore these spaces at first hand. Practitioners are well placed to stretch children's horizons by taking children on visits to explore different environments. This first-hand approach was adopted by Learning through Landscapes in their work with early years settings in Kent (Ryder Richardson forthcoming). Groups of children were taken to explore a rich outdoor environment as part of a project to make changes to their immediate outdoor spaces.

Opportunities for exploring existing spaces in new ways

Starting points

■ How could you enable young children to think about an existing space in a new way?

■ What role could an artist play in developing an outdoor area?

Practitioners may need to give young children 'permission' to think about an existing space in a new way. We found that in the child interviews children offered few suggestions for future uses of a space. Most of their answers were firmly linked to their current experiences. We asked children what they thought should happen to a rarely used piece of ground beside their play area. The quotes below illustrate children's responses:

B: Not really allowed round there.
J: Labels that say 'please don't come round here'.

(However the problem may have been our choice of the word 'should'. We discuss the role of language in the section focusing on researchers pages 97 to 104.)

Children are given permission to explore their existing space in a new way through the child-led tours. This can allow children to gain access to otherwise 'out of bounds' areas, such as hidden corners and unused ground. Safety is of course important and the adult participants on a tour need to ensure that children do not put themselves or others in danger.

Learning through Landscapes has developed another method for supporting children in thinking about an existing space in a new way. Groups of children in the Kent project were given access to a range of portable materials including cones, ropes and material in order to develop their ideas and design solutions and make plans for what could happen outside (Ryder Richardson forthcoming).

Another case study is provided by artists and a writer working with children in primary schools to redesign 'tarmac' deserts. The children were given a rich array of junk materials, chalks and fabrics to explore in the context of their playground. Exploring these textures and colours helped children to think about their existing space in a different way and formed the basis for creative new designs for the space (CABE Space 2003).

Sharing children's perspectives with parents, practitioners, councillors, planners, designers and artists

Starting points

- Which external organisations and individuals may have a role to play in changes to the outdoor environment?
- How could you find out about successful collaborative projects in your area?

The Mosaic approach makes young children's perspectives visible so that others – children and adults – can discuss meanings. One of the challenges is for practitioners to decide how this material can be shared and with whom?

We felt it was important to involve parents and all the practitioners in the Spaces to Play project as early as possible. This was our reason for displaying photographs taken during the observation in the cloakroom area during the first weeks of the project. This proved to be a good place for changing displays of the children's work during the project.

Projects involving outdoor spaces may involve other professionals who need to know about the children's views. This may include those with political power such as councillors, as well as planners, landscape architects and designers. One headteacher involved in a training session on the Mosaic approach described her intention to use this method to document the importance of the outdoor space from the children's perspectives. This nursery school had been ordered to leave their existing premises by the local authority and the headteacher was keen that there would be the support to develop the outdoor facilities at the new site.

One of the challenges is how to translate the children's perspectives into design ideas. In the Spaces to Play project this interpretation was led by a talented parent who produced the design features. A larger budget may allow other professionals to translate these ideas into practice. Working with an artist may be one possibility here (for example, Barrett 2003).

Listening to children's perspectives may lead to different concepts in design and new design questions for experts to answer. This has proved the case in the creation of the Story Garden at Discover, where primary schoolchildren and the Discover Children's Forum of children aged 4 to 11 worked with artists to create an original play space.

We have focused on the implications for using the Mosaic approach to listen to young children about institutional outdoor spaces, but what about the built environment?

■ 'New builds'

The insights provided by young children about their outdoor spaces could contribute to the design of new early years provision. There has been a rapid growth in the commissioning of new building in this sector (Sure Start 2004), including the Sure Start programme and Children's Centres. This represents an important opportunity for architects and designers to engage with young children's perspectives.

We used the Mosaic approach in our original study to find out young children's views about their indoor and outdoor environment. We found that children applied the same attention to detail to their understandings and interpretations of the indoor environment as they have to the outdoor space in the Spaces to Play project (Clark 2003).

Projects undertaken in the preschools of Reggio Emilia are leading the way in terms of architects and artists working with children's perspectives of space (for example Ceppi and Zini 1998; Reggio Children 2004).

We are developing the Mosaic approach to bring together architects and young children in the designing of the physical environment in a new project called 'Living Spaces' which began in July 2004 (funded by the Bernard van Leer Foundation). This three-year research project includes a 'new build' where the children's perspectives will play an important role throughout the process. Children's views and experiences will be gathered at the design stage, together with the views of practitioners and parents. This material will create a platform for establishing a dialogue with the architects. After the completion and occupation of the new building, children will play a central role in the review of the space.

Wider environment

We have concentrated on children's views about institutional spaces. However, in discussing with children about these specific places they have also demonstrated their knowledge and interest in the wider environment. The Mosaic approach could provide one means of enabling young children's perspectives to be included in discussions about changes to public urban and rural spaces. The visual documentation could enable young children's views to be represented at planning meetings without the need for their attendance in person.

There are numerous possibilities for making young children's perspectives of their wider environment more visible. The question is how to move towards a culture where children's views and experiences are taken seriously as a matter of course, rather than ignored as irrelevant or treated as charming but impractical (Kirby and others 2003).

▪▪ Messages for practitioners linking the
▪▪ Mosaic approach and learning

Listening and learning cannot be separated. Listening is an integral part of the learning process. The type of listening that occurs will depend on the model of learning we follow. If we see learning as a one-way process of imparting knowledge to children for them to absorb, then the focus of the listening is on the children. However, if we see learning as a transactional process (for example, Carr 2000), then multiple listening needs to take place (Rinaldi 2001b) between children and their peers, between adults and children, as well as children listening to adults.

We developed the Mosaic approach as a framework for listening to young children about the detail of their everyday lives. In doing this we have inadvertently set out a particular learning model where multiple listening is respected and valued. Here we explore how the Mosaic approach may facilitate learning, using case studies from the Spaces to Play project. We focus on three particular features of this learning process:

■ reversing the roles
■ learning styles
■ individual and group learning.

▪ Reversing the roles

We chose a photograph for the cover of our original book taken by a four-year-old, Clare, of her friend Meryl taking a photograph. It is a powerful image because the focus of the lens is firmly on the viewer. We as readers are placed under the spotlight by the children. This represents the theoretical basis of the Mosaic approach, where the traditional classroom roles between adults and children are reversed. The children are the ones with the unique knowledge to impart and debate with adults.

An example of this shifting of relationships occurred in a research project carried out using the Mosaic approach by an early years trainer. She was talking to a practitioner about a child. The practitioner commented: 'she listens if she thinks she is getting what she wants. She would like to reverse roles' (private correspondence). The trainer remarked that this was exactly what the Mosaic approach allowed this child to do. The roles were reversed and the child was able to lead the process. She particularly enjoyed giving her commentary to the visiting adult on the tour.

Reversing the roles is about shifting power. This is part of the challenge of using the Mosaic approach, because the framework acknowledges that adults do not know all the answers. This relates to theories of learning that acknowledge co-construction between adults and children (for example, Rinaldi 2001b). We will illustrate this point with an example from the map-making activity in the Spaces to Play project. Ruth and Jim are working together on producing a map of the play space using their photographs and drawings. Towards the end of the session, the development officer from Learning through Landscapes calls in to the preschool to see what is happening. The following exchanges take place (Figure 3.1):

Figure 3.1: Excerpt from transcription of map-making activity

---

Development officer: I can see that Ruth and Jim have very special things outside. I can see that you chose the prams and the buggies, and I can even see you in the picture so I know you like playing with those things, maybe. And, Jim, your favourite thing … I think your favourite thing outside might be the train. Yes? And … we have a picture of you outside with the train.

Ruth: What do I like?

Development officer: You tell me what you like. Do you like Heather with the climbing frame?

Ruth: No, I like going on [the climbing frame].

Development officer: Oh, you like going on the climbing frame.

It is interesting that Ruth is the one in control of the meaning. She uses her authority to test out the development officer's knowledge and takes great pleasure in proving her 'wrong'. Ruth is the questioner, she is the meaning-maker and the broker of information.

Meighan (2004) describes different learning systems according to how the role of the learner is represented. He describes how learners can be described as resisters, receptacles, raw material, client, partner, autonomous explorers or democratic explorers.

It seems that the young children in the Spaces to Play study are learners as explorers – whether autonomous or democratic. (We will discuss the group dimension of learning below.)

The power relationships between adults and children are part of the ongoing learning environment we create. However, there may be particular times when these power relations are heightened, such as in times of transition. When young children move from an early years setting to school or from one key worker to another, then the status of the child is diminished and the adult is in more of a position of power.

Perhaps using the Mosaic approach could help during these periods of transition by re-establishing children as 'experts in their own lives' (Langsted 1994). One way to do this may be to enable a group of children within their first half term in school to take their parents on a tour of the building. Instantly they would become the knowledgeable partners who could take their less-informed parents on an exploration of the site.

What could be some of the gains for practitioners if learning relationships were reconfigured in this way? One possibility is that, in using methods that emphasise children's meaning-making and ways of seeing, practitioners have a more informed starting point for supporting children's learning. Brooker (2002) emphasises the need for this in her study of children starting school: 'Unless adults are alert to children's own ways of seeing and understanding and representing the world to themselves, it is unlikely that the child will ever manage to identify with the school's and teacher's ways of seeing'.

But how could this work within the constraints of the Foundation Stage curriculum as it currently stands? Perhaps practitioners could use the Mosaic approach as a way of tapping into children's own knowledge and understandings as a launch pad for looking at subject areas? One result may be that practitioners find that children have already achieved early learning goals. In any case goals are more likely to be reached – and in a more inspiring way – if practitioners have a clearer idea of where the children are starting from and what are their current preoccupations and interests. *Starting Strong*, the report by the Organisation for Economic Co-operation and Development (OECD 2001) came to a similar conclusion about the curriculum: 'Indeed a more proactive policy to encourage staff to adapt the curriculum to children's needs might lead to greater creativity and child initiative'.

Learning styles

The multi-sensory nature of the tools in the Mosaic approach opens up different avenues for young children to express their perspectives. Gardner (1983) and Kolb (1984) are among those who have highlighted the range of learning styles that adults and children use to think and learn. Gardner described seven multiple intelligences in his original book, although he has since expanded this list. Winters (1995) summarise the seven intelligences as:

- plays with words (verbal/linguistic)
- plays with questions (logistical/mathematical)
- plays with pictures (visual/spatial)
- plays with music (music/rhythmic)
- plays with moving (body/kinaesthetic)
- plays with socialising (interpersonal)
- plays alone (intrapersonal)

There has been a tendency in schools to concentrate on developing verbal/linguistc intelligence at the expense of other intelligences that could be supported by different learning styles (Meighan 2004). The written word can be seen in particular to be a 'privileged language' and one that adults are often more competent in using than other 'languages'. Working with the Mosaic approach challenges adults to 're-learn' some of these other languages.

Young children who took part in the Spaces to Play project had the opportunity to explore a range of learning styles, including those using verbal/linguistic skills but with an emphasis on exercising visual/spatial, body/kinaesthetic, interpersonal and intrapersonal skills. We will explain this in more detail with reference to one of the four-year-olds who took part in the study.

Case studies: learning styles

Robert

Robert was one of the older members of the preschool, who left to start school during the research. The first piece of the Mosaic he participated in was using the camera. Taking photographs in this context was a physical activity. Robert was outside and had the opportunity to move around the space in any way he chose in order to take photographs. This requires coordination in order to focus on the subject and to manipulate the shutter, the flash and the winding on mechanism. Visual/spatial skills were important in order for Robert to select images of important things.

Book-making provided the opportunity for Robert to talk about his photographs with Alison and his friends who were gathered around the table. Here he was exercising his verbal/linguistic skills at the same time as being engaged with his peers using interpersonal skills. Robert was particularly fascinated by the index card which came with his photographs. This shows a 'thumbnail' image of each photograph in the order they were taken. Robert picked out his photographs from the pile on the table and began to match his photographs with those on the index card thus developing his logistical/mathematical thinking.

Robert next led Alison on a tour with a friend. This was very much a shared activity. The boys led Alison around the outdoor space. They conducted the tour at a fast pace, dashing, skipping and running

Figure 3.2: Case study of learning styles using the Mosaic approach

Magic Carpet:
Verbal/Linguistic
Interpersonal
Visual/Spatial

Child interview:
Verbal/Linguistic
Interpersonal
Intrapersonal

Parent and practitioner interview

Robert (age 4)

Photographs and book-making:
Body/Kinaesthetic
Visual/Spatial
Verbal/Linguistic
Interpersonal
Logistical/Mathematical

Tour and map-making
Visual/Spatial
Body/Kinaesthetic
Interpersonal
Verbal/Linguistic

between the different areas, discussing what Alison needed to see as they went.

The map-making involved a great deal of talking, exchanging ideas and deciding on priorities. Robert included drawings on the map. Thus the tours and the map-making combined had given him the opportunity to develop his body/kinaesthetic, verbal/linguistic, visual/spatial and interpersonal skills.

Robert took part in the child interviews with two girls, Ester and Linda. This was a relaxed activity which took place in the play house. Robert was able to contribute thoughtful answers to the questions, reflecting on his own experiences and reacting to the responses of his peers. His favourite activity was playing with the small cars outside. He referred to an annual outing with parents and the preschool as an activity to take part in with adults outside. He did not like 'playing dollies outside'. The interview exercised Robert's verbal/linguistic, intrapersonal and interpersonal skills.

The Magic Carpet slide-show was a group activity. Robert watched the slides several times with different children. He joined in the role-play that the children started spontaneously when images appeared of their favourite play equipment. He quickly learned the order of the slides and called out the names as each slide appeared, another display of mathematical/logistical thinking.

Robert was one of the children to sit and review the book made of the research material with Alison and Barney, the toy dog. The review was a group activity but also provided the space for Robert to reflect on his part in the project, the photographs he had taken and the verbal responses he had given. The review was thus the chance for intrapersonal learning or thinking and reflection. This process Rinaldi refers to as 'internal listening' (2001b). The whole of the Mosaic approach is intended to support children's thinking about 'What is it like to be in this place?' 'What is it like to be me here?' This takes us back to the link between listening and learning.

Throughout the study children were involved in discussing, reflecting and reassessing what it was like to be at their preschool (see Clark 2003). We referred to the following quotation in our first study: 'It's not so much a matter of eliciting children's preformed ideas and opinions, it's much more a question of enabling them to explore the ways in which they perceive the world and communicate their ideas in a way that is meaningful to them' (Tolfree and Woodhead 1999). Our subsequent work using the Mosaic approach has reinforced the importance of supporting children as explorers of their environment, their relationships and themselves.

Robert was one of the more articulate members of the preschool. Can the different learning styles used in the Mosaic approach support the explorations of less articulate children? There were children in the preschool whose speech and language delay could have rendered their 'voices' unheard in the project. This would have been the case if the only tool had been a formal interview. This question-and-answer session, despite being sensitively arranged, was too challenging for some children. However, the range of learning styles provided other opportunities for these children to explore their perspectives.

Here are two examples involving four-year-old boys, Rees and Lee.

Rees

Rees was about to start school. His verbal language skills appeared limited, in the context of the preschool. Rees was however fascinated with the cameras. He took great interest in Alison's camera and was keen to volunteer to take his own photographs. He was delighted with the results and concentrated for an extended period to make a book of his images, which included a close-up photograph of a pram filled with pebbles and photographs of groups of children and adults. He chose a photograph of the house for his cover. Rees insisted on 'writing' his own captions. The practitioners were surprised when they saw his book as he had shown little interest in experimenting with writing in the preschool.

Rees had been able to convey important features of his preschool experience through having the freedom to explore using a visual/spatial learning style. This in turn led to Rees displaying an interest in communicating through developing graphic skills as well as entering into more conversations with Alison. Rees also enjoyed taking part in the Magic Carpet slide-show. He was fascinated with the mechanics of the slide projector and expressed his delight at learning how to operate the buttons to produce a new image: 'I've got that one', he explained. When a slide appeared showing Barney he picked up the toy dog and matched him to the image on the screen. The combination of this use of tools enabled Rees to make a competent contribution to the project. However, had we relied solely on the interview he would have been another invisible child. When Alison started the interview Rees copied the questions but made no other response.

Lee

Lee was one of the quieter boys in the Spaces to Play project. He gave the impression of being detached from the activities that took place in the preschool. He appeared rarely to speak to the adults and at times resorted to aggressive behaviour to communicate with his peers. Lee was, however, particularly taken with Barney the dog. He carried Barney around and talked to the toy dog as if he was a younger sibling. When it came to the child interviews Lee used Barney as a support for communicating his points of view. Alison interviewed Lee and another boy outside and the whole interview was conducted on the move.

Figure 3.3: Full transcript of interview with Lee (aged 4)

If Barney wanted to hide outside at [the preschool] where could he go?
Lee: In the house.

If Barney wanted to sit and talk to a friend outside at [the preschool] where could he go?
Lee: On the chairs.

If Barney wanted to run and climb what could he do outside?
Lee: Splashing on that bit [the soft play area] (Lee said this while looking at Barney's boots).

If Barney wanted to be with a grown-up outside what could he do?
Lee: There, over there [soft play area].

Tell Barney about the house.
Lee: We play in the house (and begins a role-play game with another child).

Tell Barney about the fence.
Lee: Because we don't go down there.

What do you like about [the preschool]?
Lee: Playing with toys (outside).

Figure 3.3 (continued)

What don't you like about being here?
Lee: I don't not like anything.

Where is your favourite place inside?
Lee: Playing on the mat.

Where is your favourite place outside?
Lee: I don't know [then he picked up Barney and walked around the play space saying] Barney wants to go on the slide, Barney wants to go on the bike, Barney wants to lie down in the house, Barney wants to go to Burger King. [Lee to Barney] Do you want a toy?

Lee's response to this last question was interesting. He declined to answer the direct question, where is your favourite place outside, but competently demonstrated what those important places might be through Barney. He gave Barney a turn on the slide as he was talking. Lee introduces his knowledge of the wider environment by talking about a café he liked which gives toys with the children's meals.

So Lee responded well to the physical nature of the interview, and to the use of Barney to aid communication. He took an active part in a second activity, the group discussion during the Magic Carpet slide-show. Again, Barney proved to be a reassuring companion for Lee. He became very animated, sharing experiences of games he had played in the different places shown on the slides. On seeing a close-up image of an old tree trunk in the castle grounds he said, 'I like jumping off them and I like jumping on them.'

This section has raised several topics for further research into using the Mosaic approach. First, there is the question of its adaptability for children with special needs. Second, the question emerges as to whether there is a particular benefit of listening in this way for boys, linked to the different learning styles available and the use of technology. This small-scale research suggests that this may be the case but there is the need for a more wide-scale research to explore this possibility. Third, there is the question of the applicability of this approach to children from minority ethnic backgrounds. Research has shown the vast gap that can exist between school culture and home culture for such children (Brooker 2002). The Mosaic approach may be a useful way of reinforcing identity and demonstrating competency in a range of media. It was not possible to test out this hypothesis in the Spaces to Play project as the children did not include this diversity but reflected the monoculture of the locality. We will be exploring this aspect in future research.

We now turn to looking at the opportunities for individual and group learning stimulated by the Mosaic approach.

Individual and group learning

The Mosaic approach had been designed to listen to individual children rather than as a group tool. We interviewed children one at a time, for example, in the original study. However, the focus on the communal outdoor space made us consider how to gather shared knowledge as well as individual meanings. The Spaces to Play project illustrates how the Mosaic approach can provide numerous opportunities for children to explore meanings individually, in pairs and small or larger groups.

Table 3.1: Opportunities for individual and group learning

Tools and activities	Individual or group learning
Cameras	Individual with an adult
Book-making	Individual in a group context
Tours	Pairs: friendship and non-friendship pairings
Map-making	Pairs and groups up to four
Child interview	Individual, pairs or small group of three
Magic Carpet	Groups of four to twelve
Review	Pairs and small groups
Evaluation	Small groups

Table 3.1 illustrates the range of opportunities given to the children to explore their ideas with an adult, alongside a peer or friend or in a larger group.

Krechevsky and Mardell (2001) propose four features of learning groups:

- Members include adults as well as children.
- Documenting children's learning processes helps to make learning visible and shapes the learning that takes place.
- Members are engaged in the emotional and aesthetic as well as intellectual dimensions of learning.
- The focus of learning extends beyond the learning of individuals to create a collective body of knowledge.

Children worked with Alison throughout the Spaces to Play project. As we have discussed earlier, the researcher's role was not one of all-knowing adult but of interested novice. This led to a positive learning environment where mutual learning was taking place. Children were able to give 'voice' to their thoughts about the play space and the researcher gained insights into the individual and group meanings. Parents and practitioners became part of the wider learning group as discussions were opened out to consider the views and experiences of other adults.

Documentation was a key feature of the learning that was taking place. The visual nature of the book-making and maps made a platform for practitioners, parents, Alison and the children to exchange thoughts and test out understandings. The more public this documentation, the wider these discussions could become. The maps displayed in the cloakroom area were in a key position to be noticed and engaged with. The books of the children's photographs were more of a personal piece of documentation that provided an avenue of communication between parents and children, but these exchanges remained unrecorded.

The group learning included the use of different senses and learning styles, as discussed above. This involved emotional learning as children discussed their feelings about different places. The emphasis on 'What is important here?' recognised that children and adults react on an emotional level to their immediate environment. Children's choice of photographs and drawings on the maps provided the opportunity to exercise their aesthetic skills together.

The project built up a range of individual meanings about the play space at the same time as adding to a collective body of knowledge. The book-making provided one example of this fusion of meanings. Jim's book of images (see Part Two: Cameras, pages 30 to 36) was the most strikingly individual account of the play space, with every feature relating to trains. The process of children taking the photographs and making their books built up a detailed understanding of important play equipment, the roles of particular children and adults, and the value given to the natural environment. The project gathered together and made visible a range of meanings about, 'What does it mean to be in this place?' This collective knowledge was summarised in the four emerging themes: places to keep, places to expand, places to change and places to add. Within these broad understandings was a range of individual meanings, some of which conflicted with each other but which had been discussed together. It was as if the range of tools in the Mosaic approach allowed children and adults to look at their play space through both ends of the 'binoculars': the close-up and individual view and the wider, more general shared perspectives.

Case study: individual and group learning

Ruth and Jim were not particular friends but both enjoyed adult company and tended to be the first to ask to join in an activity. They both were confident at discussing their views but were perhaps less at ease playing with other children. The Spaces to Play project enabled Ruth and Jim to share their carefully worked out understandings of the play space with each other and with Alison and other adults.

We will focus on the tour that Ruth and Jim led to illustrate the collaborative process in action. The tour took place on a morning after it had rained overnight. The rest of the children were playing inside. Ruth had chosen to have the camera and Jim had the tape recorder in a small bag, with the clip mike. Alison had her own camera and a notebook. The children's tour of the outdoor space incorporated the following stops:

- the caterpillar
- patch of earth
- decking
- the house
- leaves
- tangled-up bikes
- shed door.

Ruth was more of a leader than Jim and tended to be the one who suggested the next stop. However, the discussions included a range of exchanges between both children and Alison and occasionally with each other. This excerpt (Figure 3.5) is taken from the part of the conversation that took place in the house. Ruth asked to take a photograph inside the house and Alison and Jim followed.

Figure 3.4: Case study of individual and group learning using the Mosaic approach

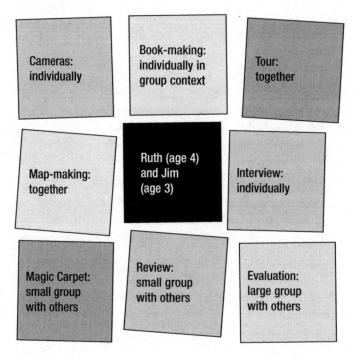

Figure 3.5: Excerpt from transcript of tour

Alison: Oh right, so we are going to go into the house. I wanted to ask you two about the house. I wanted to ask you two about here because I'm not sure, because I'm a grown-up, what happens in the house. What kinds of things happen in the house?

Ruth: Play.

Jim: When you are a train you have to get inside and get off.

Alison: And when do you like it in the house?

Jim: We play with the food.

Alison: Oh do you? What kind of food?

Jim: The ones in the house …

[meanwhile Ruth has been taking photos of us in the house]

Ruth: How about you?

Alison: How about me? How do you mean, how about me?

Ruth: Take a picture …

Alison: Yes, I'm going to take a picture, oh … that was a close one, I've had some very funny photos taken of me (here) … Now I still want to find out about this house? Do you always like playing in the house or sometimes?

Jim: Sometimes when there is no more a lot in there (pause)

Alison: When there is no more a lot in there, is that right?

Jim: Yes.

[Ruth leads Alison and Jim outside and takes a picture of the leaves on the table.]

Ruth suggested visiting the house and is in charge of making the visual record, which she does competently. Meanwhile Jim demonstrates his knowledge about the house and the role-play he enjoys there (hiding under the table as a train). Alison's questions seem a bit persistent. However, Jim patiently continues and conveys an important piece of information, which adds to the collective knowledge about the house: children don't like it when the house gets overcrowded. Other children confirmed this in the child interviews and the practitioner interviews revealed overcrowding as a serious concern.

The researcher's role changes during the tour just as the children take on different roles, sometimes taking the lead in the dialogue and at other times directing the camera. The researcher is at times the uninformed novice, for example in the comment above: 'I wanted to ask you two about here because I'm not sure, because I'm a grown-up, what happens in the house.'

At other times the researcher supports or 'scaffolds' the children's learning, for example in the use of the cameras. She models behaviour by taking her own photographs, praises the children when they have mastered the winding on technology and instructs them on how to use the flash.

This example illustrates how the distinctions become blurred between research and teaching. Seidel (2001) discusses this in relation to roles within the preschools of Reggio Emilia and the Project Zero American research study: 'The actions of instruction, assessment, documentation and research come to contain each other. They cannot be pulled apart in any practical sense; they are a piece. No dichotomy between teaching and research remains.'

We need to keep in mind this blurring of boundaries when coming to the next section on messages for researchers on using the Mosaic approach. Many of the questions raised are relevant to practitioners too.

The researcher and children taking part in the review
(Photo by Gail Ryder Richardson)

Messages for researchers using the Mosaic approach with young children

The Spaces to Play project is the second time we have worked with a group of young children using the Mosaic approach. However, since developing the approach we have conducted training workshops and corresponded with others who have adapted the Mosaic approach to carry out research with young children. In this section we will focus on some of the research issues that have emerged from this project and from comments from others with direct experience of trying these methods.

What about the role of researcher using the Mosaic approach?

The researcher is allowed to play the part of 'authentic novice' by using the Mosaic approach. This 'novice role' is easier perhaps for a researcher who is new to a research setting than for a practitioner working with children she or he knows well. The researcher is genuinely less informed of the details of a particular play environment than children who have played in that space for many months. This allows the children to demonstrate their competence or expertise, while the researcher can enjoy being guided by the children. Tammivaara and Enright (1986, quoted in Carr 2000: 46) refer to the researcher as 'playing dumb (implying that the researcher needs help and guidance)'.

Some of the older four-year-olds had been attending the preschool in the Spaces to Play project for two years. They had spent up to 10 sessions a week for three terms a year in this environment and thus were intimately acquainted with the space both inside and outside. The children were happy to accept the researcher as a novice or an adult who obviously needed help to find out about their place.

This role as novice echoes the role reversal we have discussed in relation to practitioners in the previous section. The researcher has accepted a less powerful role in order for the young children to be able to take more control of the research agenda. We have begun with a focus on an area of interest but there is scope within the Mosaic approach for children to introduce new directions. This was demonstrated in the Spaces to Play project by the boy who included photographs of inside spaces in his book of photographs of the outside. We had stated our interest in the outdoor environment but that did not stop him illustrating the importance of both indoor and outdoor spaces.

Is there an advantage of an outsider using the Mosaic approach rather than an insider – a practitioner who knows the children and the setting well? There appear to be advantages and disadvantages either way. We have discussed here the advantages for researchers of the role of 'novice'. However, one disadvantage for researchers is that they do not have a long-term relationship with the children that would enable them to use their insights into children's priorities and interests in the children's ongoing learning. Perhaps the key question is not about who is doing the listening but about what is the individual's expectations of the children and what skills and resources they have at their disposal to support children's self-expression?

The role of researcher using the Mosaic approach is in complete contrast to a researcher carrying out a psychological test on young children in a laboratory.

This traditional way of listening to children places the researcher firmly in the expert's chair with the child as object. Many of these tests rely on children producing the 'right' answer. This contrasts with the view of the child promoted by the sociology of childhood, where children are seen as active subjects in research, where research needs to be with children and not 'on' children (see, for example, Christensen and James 2000; Lewis and others 2003). Participatory methods, including the Mosaic approach, treat children as active participants in research and make it easier for children to 'sit in the expert's chair'. This could lead to a reframing of some of the dominant research questions concerned with early years services. For example, what are the possibilities for listening to young children as active participants around the contentious issue of whether nursery is 'bad' for children?

◼ What about the time it takes?

Research which involves children and particularly younger children will take a surprising amount of time to carry out. Time is an important factor in planning at the preparation stage, while carrying out the fieldwork, and in the analysis and writing-up stage. This time factor applies to others involved in listening to young children, whether they are early years practitioners or other professionals who have less direct contact with children.

Preparation

Getting to know the setting and the children is a crucial part of using the Mosaic approach and other qualitative methods. It is of particular importance because children need to feel comfortable talking to you and working with you. A wary child is unlikely to demonstrate their competencies. Talking to practitioners at all levels within an early years setting is part of this preparation. Once permission has been gained for carrying out research in a particular context it is important that practitioners working directly with the children, as well as the manager, are aware of who the researcher is and what is the purpose of the research. It may help children to be at ease with the researcher if the other adults present are able to welcome them. The children may be engaged in other research projects so it is important to check this at an early stage.

Fieldwork

Listening to young children's views and experiences cannot be rushed. One indication of this is when young children say to a researcher 'I don't know.' This can be an indication that the questioner is approaching the task in an unhelpful or rushed way rather than that the children are unable to give a reply. Over the hundred and more conversations Alison had with the children during the Spaces to Play project, only once or twice did a child say to her, 'I don't know.' They were able to display a great deal of knowledge about their environment, but this did take time and patience.

Young children need time to experience a new activity, resource or experience before any research purpose is explored. This was clearly illustrated when using the Magic Carpet tool. The children were fascinated by seeing a corner of their classroom turned into a darkened tent. The two days allocated for this activity did not allow the children enough time to explore this new space before the slides were introduced, which heightened their level of excitement and probably reduced their ability to focus on the subject. Ideally, the children would have benefited from having a week to explore the tent, and then being introduced to the slide projector, so they could explore their own shadows before being introduced to the slides.

The multi-method approach is time-consuming. It would be far quicker to use one or two tools. However, it is drawing together the information gathered from different sources that enables a more in-depth picture to be produced, and allows children of different abilities to make a contribution to the research.

The ongoing documentation that is a feature of the Mosaic approach takes time to organise. Making displays of photographs after the observation in the Spaces to Play project was an important way of including children, practitioners and parents, but did require extra effort. Similarly, the making and duplicating of the children's photobooks and the assembling of the maps requires intensive work and careful record-keeping.

Analysis, writing up and dissemination

One of the advantages and disadvantages of a multi-method approach is the mass of research material that is generated. There is an added time factor in analysing each of the tools. It can feel like sifting sand. This is partly because, when gathering material with young children, their interests and preoccupations will undoubtedly be at times different from those of the researcher. This can lead to many hours of conversation with occasional 'nuggets' of information about the researcher's original interest.

The book-making activity in the Spaces to Play project was one example of this. There were many hours of audiotape recorded while the book-making was in progress. There was the added difficulty of recordings being made in a preschool setting with a high level of background and sometimes foreground noise. The main focus of the children's conversations was around using the glue sticks rather than on the subject of the photographs. The new task of manipulating the glue sticks (rather than using liquid PVA glue applied with a spatula) represented a challenge that required concentration and discussion alongside the adult focus on selecting photographs. This could be the focus of a research study (see Carr 2000). One question for researchers is how flexible can we be in our research agenda. Maybe we would gain more insights or 'nuggets' by following the children's preoccupations.

Research that draws on visual and verbal material requires time in order to prepare examples of different modes of communication at the report stage and in further dissemination. There is the additional task of checking consent for the use of children's photographs in subsequent publications.

What about the language we choose?

Talking and listening to young children requires great attention to how we phrase our questions and explain our interests. This applies in the Mosaic approach to both the informal questions we ask as part of working with the individual tools and the child interviews.

Carr (2000: 45) refers to a number of researchers who have been brave enough to share examples of unsuccessful interviews with preschool children. Hatch (1990) asks a young child: 'What do you like doing best in the housekeeping corner?' The girl's responses imply she is trying to second-guess the 'answer': 'Play dress-up ... Is it computer?' This example shows how the way we phrase questions is linked to the role the child expects the researcher to be playing.

Young children can interpret questions in a literal way. We tried a question in the Spaces to Play project in which the children's responses surprised us. The question was: 'What is missing outside at [your preschool]?' Some of the children's responses were more literal than we had anticipated. Children who were answering the questions while sitting in the play house answered 'the window'. The perspex was missing because a vandal had broken the pane and it had to be removed. This illustrates how we need to pilot and review the questions we use and to consider the immediate context in which we may be asking the questions. 'What is missing here?' illustrates how we, as adults, can condense a complex concept into a seemingly straightforward question. This question used simple words but was in fact complicated. What we were aiming at here was: 'In view of your experience of this and other play spaces what resources or opportunities should be added to this preschool's outdoor space?'

Perhaps, as researchers, we need to consider more carefully what are our explicit and implicit purposes when asking each question, and what demands this makes on our interviewees.

Why use a toy as an intermediary?

We decided to use Barney, the toy dog, as part of the research strategy in the Spaces to Play project. We would not see this as a necessary element of research with young children but as a possible support for the researcher as novice. In the particular preschool we were working in, the children quickly accepted the role of the toy as another visitor. We found that there were particular children who were especially attracted to Barney. This included both girls and boys in the group. Several children photographed him and included him in their photobooks. There were a number of children who seemed happier talking to Barney than to the researcher. This included one child, Lee (see above), who was reticent when talking to Alison on the tour but picked Barney up and talked to him

In some research contexts, a toy may be an unnecessary extra, which distracts the children or the researcher from the intended purpose (Cameron and Clark 2004). However, there may be certain research contexts and individual children who respond well to this device.

Perhaps this is one example of the need to be flexible in relation to the personalities, abilities and cultures of different children. Gollop (2000) discusses the need for 'flexibility, sensitivity and adaptability' when interviewing children.

This may mean that, for some researchers working with particular children, a toy or puppet is an added bonus, whereas with other children in different circumstances a toy is not necessary. The researcher would, however, need to feel at ease with this way of working, otherwise the children would be unlikely to take to the toy.

Could the Mosaic approach be used in research with older children?

The Mosaic approach has been developed to facilitate communication between young children and adults about children's perspectives. The research studies have demonstrated how three- and four-year-olds can provide insights into the complex individual and collective views of their world. The research suggests that this approach may offer possibilities for working with older children and adults.

Children's abilities to communicate using a range of visual and verbal languages is not limited to the early years. However, their skills and confidence in working with these different languages will change according to their developing talents and the support or constraints of their learning environment. The Mosaic approach could offer a framework for older children to explore, 'What does it mean for me to be in this place?' In fact, this is a question that adults of different ages and children could explore in this visual way, particularly those children or adults who would benefit from expressing their views and experiences in non-verbal ways. The starting points would need to include:

- a view of the child or adult as 'experts in their own lives'
- tools that played to the participants' strengths (rather than to the researcher's strengths)
- a willingness to construct a platform of communication for children and adults to discuss meanings together.

Perhaps there are possibilities here for making visible the views and experiences of older children in particular circumstances where their perspectives may be hidden. Children involved in adoption or fostering may be one such group.

The tools have been chosen to work with young children. However, elements such as the cameras could be easily modified to match the skills of older children, such as making a short film of the tour.

In Part Three, we have looked at the messages for practitioners and researchers in using the Mosaic approach. We have raised the issue that the boundaries between these roles may become blurred. Possibilities for developing this approach include exploring the contribution young children could make to changes to their indoor and outdoor environments, such as new builds.

We have looked in detail at the potential for using this multi-method framework for including the 'voices' of children with different needs through the various learning styles and raised the possibility of using this approach with older children and adults.

We have examined the possibilities for using the Mosaic approach to promote a range of learning situations for children and adults, including work as individuals, in pairs and in small and larger groups.

Issues of time, negotiating meanings and the choice of language are common to both practitioners and researchers. Importantly, the reversal of roles between adults and children presents challenges for those working in early childhood institutions and for researchers in an academic context.

Conclusion

We have explored the complex question of how to listen to young children's thoughts about their outdoor environment. We have focused on a real-life example to illustrate how young children can be supported in exploring their views on, and experiences of, their outdoor spaces. Listening has been at the centre of this project, not a shallow, passive one-way exercise between an adult and a child but listening as a multilayered, vibrant process. Rinaldi (2001b) describes this as multiple listening: 'This concept of a "context of multiple listening" overturns the traditional teaching–learning relationship; the focus shifts to learning – children's self-learning, and the learning achieved by the group of children and adults together'.

This self-learning and group learning enabled both individual and collective knowledge to be created.

One of the challenges of this approach is, where do these new insights lead? The Spaces to Play project contributed to changes at a practical and theoretical level.

First, the project provided children's insights and promoted dialogue with parents and practitioners that led to positive changes to the outdoor environment and to children's access to those spaces. Second, at a theoretical level the practitioners raised their expectations of the children and reconsidered ways of rearranging their planning to enable children's capabilities and interests to become more visible. This raises possibilities about how the Mosaic approach might be one way of enabling children's current occupations to be acknowledged and given status within the constraints of a fixed curriculum.

But could this collective knowledge have a wider implication beyond the early years institution? This raises the question of who else may need to be involved in this multiple listening in order for young children's perspectives to feature in the outdoor environment? Architects, planners, councillors and politicians are several of the powerful groups that need to be brought into discussion with young children about, 'What does it mean to be in this place?' Documentation and the Mosaic approach present one possibility for making this a reality.

Appendix A:

Child interview schedule

1. I am ....
2. I am ... years old
3. If Barney wanted to hide outside at the preschool where could he go?
4. If Barney wanted to sit and talk to a friend outside at the preschool where could he go?
5. If Barney wanted to run and climb what could he do outside?
6. If Barney wanted to be with a grown-up outside what could he do?
7. Tell Barney about the house.
8. Tell Barney about the fence.
9. What do you like about the preschool?
10. What don't you like about being here?
11. Where is your favourite place inside?
12. Where is your favourite place outside?
13. Where don't you like outside?
14. What would you like to do more often outside at the preschool?
15. What is missing outside at the preschool?
16. What do you think should happen on the grassy parts of the preschool?
17. Is there anything else Barney needs to know about the preschool?

Thank you very much.

Appendix B:

Practitioner's interview schedule

1. What do you think children gain from playing outside at the preschool?
2. Where do you think are the children's favourite places outside?
3. Where do you think they don't like?
4. Where might they go to hide?
5. Where might they go to sit and talk to their friends?
6. Where might they go to run and climb?
7. What do you enjoy doing with the children outside?
8. Tell me about how the children use the house.
9. What do you think is missing outside at the preschool?
10. What would you like to give away?
11. What would you like to be able to put out everyday at the preschool?
12. Any other changes you would like to make?

Thank you very much.

Appendix C:

Parent's interview schedule

1. How long has your son/daughter been coming to the preschool?
2. What does [child] enjoy doing at home inside and outside?
3. What do you think would be a good day for her/him at the preschool?
4. What do you think would be a bad day for her/him at the preschool?
5. Do you think [child] enjoys being outside at the preschool?
6. What do you think they enjoy doing outside here?
7. Any thing you think [child] doesn't like about being outside here?
8. Are there any changes you would like to see to the outside?

Thank you very much.

References

Adams, E and Ingham, S (1998) *Changing Places: Children's participation in environmental planning*. London: Children's Society.

Barrett, K (2003) 'Running wild', *Early Education*, Summer, 3–4.

Bilton, H (2002) *Outdoor Play in the Early Years: Management and innovation*, 2nd edn. London: David Fulton.

Borland, M (2001) *Improving Consultation with Children in Relevant Aspects of Policy Making and Legislation in Scotland*. Edinburgh: Scottish Parliament.

Brooker, L (2002) *Starting School – Young Children's Learning Cultures*. Buckingham: Open University Press.

Bruner, J (1985) 'Models of the learner', *Educational Researcher*, 14, 6, 5–8.

Burke, C (2003) 'Play in focus: children's photographic survey of their own sites of play', research paper, School of Education, University of Leeds. http://www.education.leeds.ac.uk/%7Eeducb/play/ (accessed October 2004).

CABE Space (2003) *What Would You Do with Space?* London: CABE Space.

Cameron, C and Clark, A (2004) *Video Observation Study of Childcare Work: UK National Report*, unpublished report, Thomas Coram Research Unit, Institute of Education, University of London.

Carr, M 'Seeking children's perspectives about their learning', in Smith, A, Taylor, NJ and Gollop, M (eds) (2000) *Children's Voices: Research, policy and practice*. Auckland: Pearson Education.

Ceppi, G and Zini, M (1998) *Children's Spaces and Relations: Metaproject for the environment of young children*. Domus Academy Research Center: Reggio Children.

Chawla, L (ed.) (2002) *Growing up in an Urbanising World*. Paris and London: UNESCO Publishing/Earthscan Publications.

Children's Play Council (2002) *More than Swings and Roundabouts: planning for outdoor play*. London: Children's Play Council.

Christensen, P and James, A (eds) (2000) *Research with Children*. London: Falmer Press.

Clark, A 'The Mosaic approach and research with young children', in Lewis, V and others (eds) (2003) *The Reality of Research with Children and Young People*. London: Sage.

Clark, A (2004) *Listening as a Way of Life: Why and How We Listen to Young Children*. London: National Children's Bureau for DFES.

Clark, A 'Talking and listening to children', in Dudek, D (ed.) (forthcoming) *Landscapes of Childhood*. London: Architectural Press.

Clark, A, McQuail, S and Moss, P (2003) *Exploring the Field of Listening to and Consulting with Young Children*, Research Report 445. London: DfES.

Clark, A and Moss, P (2001) *Listening to Young Children: The Mosaic approach*. London: National Children's Bureau for the Joseph Rowntree Foundation.

Clark, A, Moss, P and Kjørholt, A (eds) (forthcoming) *Beyond Listening: Children's perspectives on early childhood services*. Bristol: Policy Press.

Cousins, J (1999) *Listening to Four-Year-Olds: How they can help us plan their education and care*. London: National Early Years Network.

Cutler, D and Frost, R (2001) *Taking the Initiative: Promoting young people's involvement in public decision-making in the UK*. York: Carnegie Young People's Initiative.

David, T and others (2003) *Birth to three matters: a review of the literature compiled to inform the Framework. Research report 444.* London: DfES.

Daycare Trust (1998*) Listening to Children: Young children's views on childcare: A guide for parents*. London: Daycare Trust.

Dickins, M (2004) *Listening as a way of life: listening to young disabled children.* London: National Children's Bureau for DfES.

Dickins, M, Emerson, S and Gordon-Smith, P (2003) *Starting with Choice: Inclusive strategies for consulting young children*. London: Save the Children.

Driscoll, V (2004) 'Creative Artists in the Outdoors', *Early Education*, 42, Spring, 7–9.

Driskell, D (2002) *Creating Better Cities with Children and Youth*. Paris and London: UNESCO Publishing/Earthscan Publications.

Dudek, M (2000) *Kindergarten Architecture: Space for the imagination*, 2nd edn. London: Spon Press.

Dupree, E, Bertram, T and Pascal, C (2001) 'Listening to children's perspectives of their early childhood settings', paper presented at EECERA Conference 2001.

Edwards, C, Gandini, L and Foreman, G (eds) (1998) *The Hundred Languages of Children: The Reggio Emilia approach to early childhood education*. New Jersey: Ablex Publishing Corporation.

Entz, S and Galarza, SL (2000) *Picture This: Digital and instant photography activities for early childhood learning*. Thousand Oaks, CA: Corwin Press.

Gardner, H (1983) *Frames of Mind: A Theory of Multiple Intelligences*. London: Fontana.

Gollop, M 'Interviewing children: a research perspective', in Smith, A, Taylor, NJ and Gollop, M (eds) (2000) *Children's Voices: research, policy and practice*. Auckland: Pearson Education.

Hart, R (1979) *Children's Experience of Place*. New York: Irvington Publishers Inc.

Hart, R (1997) *Children's Participation*. London: Earthscan.

Hatch, J (1990) 'Young children as informants in classroom studies', *Early Childhood Research Quarterly* 5, 251–64.

Hood, S (2004) *The Second State of London's Children Report*. London: Office of the Children's Rights Commissioner for London.

Hood, S (2001) *State of London's Children Report*. London: Office of the Children's Rights Commissioner for London.

James, A and Prout, A (1997) *Constructing and Reconstructing Childhood*, 2nd edn. London: Falmer Press.

Johnson, V, Ivan Smith, E, Gordon, G, Pridmore, P and Scott, P (eds) (1998) *Stepping Forward: Children and young people's participation in the development process*. London: Intermediate Technology.

Kirby, P, Lanyon, C, Cronin, K and Sinclair, R (2003) *Building a Culture of Participation: Involving children and young people in policy, service planning, delivery and evaluation*. London: DfES.

Kolb, D (1984) *Experiential Learning: Experience as the Source of Learning and Development*. Englewood Cliffs, NJ: Prentice Hall.

Krechevsky, M and Mardell, B 'Four features of learning in groups', in Giudici, C, Rinaldi, C and Krechevsky, M (2001) *Making Learning Visible: Children as individual and group learners*. Reggio Emilia: Reggio Children.

Lancaster, P (2003) *Listening to Young Children*. Maidenhead: Open University Press.

Langsted, O 'Looking at quality from the child's perspective', in Moss, P and Pence, A (eds) (1994) *Valuing Quality in Early Childhood Services: New approaches to defining quality*. London: Paul Chapman Publishing.

Lansdown, G 'The UN Convention on the Rights of the Child – Progress in the UK', in Nutbrown, C (ed.) (1996) *Children's Rights and Early Education*. London: Paul Chapman.

Lewis, V, Kellett, M, Robinson, C, Fraser, S and Ding, S (eds) (2003) *The Reality of Research with Children and Young People*. London: Sage.

MacNaughton, G (2003) *Shaping Early Childhood: Learners, curriculum and contexts.* London: Sage.

Mayall, B (2002) *Towards a Sociology for Childhood: Thinking from children's lives.* Buckingham: Open University Press.

McLarnon, J (2004) *Listening as a Way of Life: Supporting Parents and Carers to Listen. A Guide for Practitioners.* London: National Children's Bureau for DfES.

McMillan, M (1919) *The Nursery School.* London: Dent.

Meighan, R (2004) 'Natural learning and the next learning system', Paper presented at the 7th Annual Playlink/Portsmouth City Council Conference, March.

Miller, J (1997) *Never too Young: how young children can take responsibility and make decisions.* London: National Early Years Network/Save the Children.

NSPCC/Triangle (2004) *All Join In.* London: NSPCC.

OECD (2001) *Starting Strong: Early childhood education and care.* Paris: Organisation for Economic Co-operation and Development.

Ouvry, M (2003) *Exercising Muscles and Minds: Outdoor play and the early years curriculum.* London: National Children's Bureau.

Parker, C 'When is she coming back?', in Abbott, L and Nutbrown, C (eds) (2001) *Experiencing Reggio Emilia: Implications for pre-school provision.* Buckingham: Open University Press.

Perry, J (2001) *Outdoor Play: Teaching strategies with young children.* New York: Teacher College Press.

Petrie, P, Egharevba, I, Oliver, C and Poland, G (2000) *Out-of-school Lives, Out-of-school Services.* London: Stationery Office.

QCA (2000) *Curriculum Guidance for the Foundation Stage.* London: Qualifications and Curriculum Authority.

Qvortrup, J, Bardy, M, Sgritta, G and Wintersberger, H (eds) (1994) *Childhood Matters: social theory, practice and policy.* Aldershot: Avebury.

Reggio Children (2004) *Children, Art, Artists*. Reggio Emilia: Reggio Children.

Rich, D (2004) *Listening as a Way of Life: Listening to Babies*. London: National Children's Bureau for DfES.

Rinaldi, C (2001a) 'A pedagogy of listening', *Children in Europe*, 1, 2–5.

Rinaldi, C (2001b) 'Documentation and assessment: what is the relationship?', pp. 78–89 in Giudici, C, Rinaldi, C and Krechevsky, M (2001) *Making Learning Visible: Children as individual and group learners*. Reggio Emilia: Reggio Children.

Road, N (2004) *Listening as a Way of Life. Are Equalities an Issue? Finding Out What Young Children Think*. London: National Children's Bureau for DfES.

Rowe, S (1991) *The Seasons in the School Grounds*. Winchester: Learning through Landscapes.

Ryder Richardson, G (forthcoming) *'Creating a Space to Grow': developing outdoor learning environments for very young children*. London: David Fulton.

Seidel, S 'Perspectives on research in education', pp. 330–5 in Giudici, C, Rinaldi, C and Krechevsky, M (2001) *Making Learning Visible: Children as individual and group learners*. Reggio Emilia: Reggio Children.

Smith, F and Barker, J (1999) 'From Ninja Turtles to the Spice Girls: Children's participation in the development of out of school play environments', *Built Environment*, 25, 1, 35–46.

Stirling Council (2000) *Inside Out and Outside In*. Stirling: Children's Services, Stirling.

Sure Start (2002) *Birth to Three Matters – A framework to support children in their earliest years*. London: Sure Start, DfES.

Sure Start (2004) *Building for Sure Start: Integrated provision for under fives*. Client guide and design guide. London: Sure Start, DfES.

Taamivaara, J and Enright, D (1986) 'On eliciting Information: dialogues with child informants', *Anthropology and Education Quarterly*, 17, 218–38.

Titman, W (1994) *Special Places for Special People – Hidden curriculum of school grounds*. Godalming: World Wide Fund for Nature.

Tolfree, D and Woodhead, M (1999) 'Tapping a key resource', *Early Childhood Matters*, 91, 19–23.

Vygotsky, L (1978) 'The role of play in development', in Cole, M, John-Steiner, V, Scribner, S and Souberman, E (eds and trans) *Minds in Society*. Cambridge, MA: Harvard University Press.

Wigfall, V and Moss, P (2001) *More than the Sum of its Parts? A study of a multi-agency childcare network*. London: National Children's Bureau.

Winters, E 1995. *Seven Styles of Learning.* http://www.bena.com/ewinters/styles.html *(accessed January 2004).*

Available from NCB Book Sales

Listening to Four Year Olds
How they can help us plan their education and care
Jacqui Cousins

This book considers:
- What are four-year-olds really saying when they talk, or refuse to talk, to us?
- What can early years workers learn from four-year-olds' words and silences?
- How can the views of four-year-olds be used in the day-to-day planning of their care and education?

Published by the National Early Years Network. 2003. 72pp. ISBN 1 870985 50 8. Price £10.50. NCB members £8.

Listening to Young Children
The Mosaic approach
Alison Clark and Peter Moss

The Mosaic approach is a multi-method approach in which children's own photographs, tours and maps can be joined to talking and observing to gain a deeper understanding of children's perspectives on their early childhood settings.

Published for the Joseph Rowntree Foundation by NCB. 2001. 88pp. ISBN 1 900990 62 8. Price £12.95. NCB members £10.95.

Quality in Diversity in Early Learning
A framework for early childhood practitioners, 2nd edition
Early Childhood Forum

This framework makes a stand for the unequivocal entitlement of all children to high-quality care and education in whatever provision they are placed. It enables early childhood practitioners to think about, understand, support and extend the learning of children from birth to eight.

2003. 114pp. ISBN 1 904787 07 X. Price £18. NCB members £12.50.

Relationships and Learning
Caring for children from birth to three
Anna Gillespie Edwards

Based on observations of children in daycare settings, *Relationships and Learning* highlights the importance of one-to-one relationships with young children for fostering their self-esteem, well-being and ability to learn

2002. 112pp. ISBN 1 900990 75 X. Price £16.50. NCB members £11.50.

To order:
- post your order to Book Sales, National Children's Bureau, 8 Wakley Street, London EC1V 7QE
- fax your order to 020 7843 6087
- phone 020 7843 6029/8 to order by credit/debit card

For orders up to £28 add £4 for p&p. For orders £28 and over, add 15% of the total order for p&p. For orders below £28, please include payment with order.